STUDY GUIDE
FOR
SELL AND SELL SHORT

Books by Dr. Alexander Elder

Trading for a Living
Study Guide for Trading for a Living

Rubles to Dollars:
   Making Money on Russia's Exploding Financial Frontier

Come into My Trading Room
Study Guide for Come into My Trading Room

Straying from the Flock: Travels in New Zealand

Entries & Exits: Visits to Sixteen Trading Rooms
Study Guide for Entries & Exits

STUDY GUIDE
FOR
SELL AND SELL SHORT

Dr. Alexander Elder
www.elder.com

WILEY

John Wiley & Sons, Inc.

For general information on our other products and services or for technical support, please contact our Customer Care Department within the United States at
(800) 762-2974, outside the United States at (317) 572-3993 or fax (317) 572-4002.

Wiley also publishes its books in a variety of electronic formats. Some content
that appears in print may not be available in electronic books. For more information about Wiley products, visit our web site at www.wiley.com.

ISBN 978-0-470-20047-6

Printed in the United States of America

10 9 8 7 6 5 4 3 2 1

CONTENTS

ABOUT THIS STUDY GUIDE

I t feels exciting to discover an attractive stock and watch it go vertical after you buy. It is just as exciting to see it collapse soon after you short. This joy is only a small part of the game.

You can expect to spend the bulk of your time doing your homework. At times you might scan a long list of stocks and not find anything particularly attractive. At other times you may find a stock that you like but your money management rules will not allow you to buy. Or you can put on a trade in moments but spend half an hour documenting it in your diary. The toil of homework takes up the bulk of a serious trader's time. Whoever said "success is 10% inspiration and 90% perspiration" must have come through Wall Street.

I created this *Study Guide* to help you prepare for the road ahead. My goal was to point out some of the best opportunities, flag some of the worst risks, and get you into the habit of tracking your performance. I often say to my students, "Show me a trader with good records, and I will show you a good trader." I hope this *Study Guide* will help you acquire the habit of asking hard questions, testing all ideas on your own data, and keeping good notes.

This book is divided into three sections. The first focuses on buying, managing money, and keeping records; the second on selling; and the third on selling short. Each section, in turn, consists of two parts. In the beginning, there are textual questions, and towards the end there are visual questions, with charts that require you to make trading decisions. Each section concludes with a scale to help you gauge your performance.

I took great care in crafting the answers in the back of the book. I wanted to go beyond merely saying that A was right and B was wrong—I wanted to explain the reasons behind the answers. Because of these extensive comments, the Answers section of this *Study Guide* serves as an extension of the main book, *Sell and Sell Short.*

Please do not rush through this book. Trading is a marathon, not a 100-yard dash. Take your time to think and work through a few questions each day. After you have worked through the entire *Study Guide* and rated your performance, put it aside for two or three months, then pick it up again and retake the tests to see whether your grades have improved. Trading is like so many other serious pursuits—the more you put into it, the more you will get out of it.

Trading is a lonely business, which is why I encourage traders to connect with others and share research and learning. Some of my students have become good friends, and here I want to acknowledge the contribution of Jeff Parker, a camper and a member of the Spike group. He reviewed and critiqued both *Sell and Sell Short* and this *Study Guide.* Jeff is a very kind guy, but an extremely hard man to please. He made dozens of critical comments which helped me improve this book. This manuscript would have been finished sooner and with less pain if I had not shown it to Jeff, but the book came out better thanks to him. Now, by picking up this *Study Guide* and facing its hard questions you have made the same choice as I did. When we expose ourselves to the risk of criticism, we become stronger.

I cordially wish you success in your trading career.

Dr. Alexander Elder
New York City, 2008

QUESTIONS

How to Buy, Manage Risk, & Keep Records

Wwhen I sat down to write a book about selling, it soon became clear that it had to begin with a section on buying and all that relates to it. Beginners buy when some vague tips float their way. Experienced traders know that serious buying requires serious research.

Scanning the stock market and researching individual stocks is very important, but analysis alone will not make you a successful trader. Serious buying requires good money management. There are simple mathematical rules that tell you how much risk you may accept on any individual trade as well as on all your open trades combined. Those who violate risk limits have a very short life expectancy in the markets.

There are certain psychological rules that can help you make your life in the markets less stressful and more satisfying and profitable. And there are certain highly desirable ways of record-keeping that will help you grow into a mature and successful trader.

You have to buy well in order to sell well.

That is why, before we discuss selling and shorting, you need to answer important questions about psychology and money management, buying decisions, and record-keeping.

Please do not rush as you work through this chapter. A house is only as strong as its foundation. Please answer these questions with a great deal of thought and record them on the Answer Sheet on pages 4 and 5. Re-read the appropriate sections in *Sell and Sell Short* if you miss any answers.

Answer Sheet

Questions	Max. Pts. Available	Trial 1	Trial 2	Trial 3	Trial 4	Trial 5	Trial 6
1	1						
2	1						
3	1						
4	1						
5	1						
6	1						
7	1						
8	1						
9	1						
10	1						
11	1						
12	1						
13	1						
14	1						
15	1						
16	1						
17	1						
18	1						
19	1						
20	1						
21	1						
22	1						
23	1						
24	1						
25	1						
26	1						

(continuing)

Answer Sheet, *continued*

Questions	Max. Pts. Available	Trial 1	Trial 2	Trial 3	Trial 4	Trial 5	Trial 6
27	1						
28	1						
29	1						
30	1						
31	1						
32	1						
33	1						
34	1						
35	1						
36	1						
Total points	36						

Question 1—The Stress of Holding a Position

Having bought a stock, most people find themselves in the least stressful position if that stock:

1. Rises slightly
2. Skyrockets
3. Declines slightly
4. Collapses

Question 2—Your Trading Edge

Your trading edge can come from:

1. Fundamental analysis
2. Technical studies
3. Discipline
4. All of the above

Question 3—The Three Great Divides

The three great divides in trading include all of the following, except:

1. Technical vs. fundamental research
2. Trend vs. counter-trend trading
3. Relying on TV news vs. an advisory service
4. Discretionary vs. systematic trading

Question 4—Price and Value

Find the incorrect statement about the relationship between price and value:

1. Values change slowly, prices change fast.
2. Studying earnings reports and industry trends allows you to discover value.
3. Moving averages help define the value zone by tracking public consensus.
4. Price equals value at any given moment.

Question 5—Fundamental and Technical Analysis

Which of the following statements about fundamental and technical analysis is incorrect?

1. A fundamentalist calculates the value of the business that issued a stock.
2. Having precise information about the fundamentals tells you exactly which way a stock is going to go.
3. A technician looks for repetitive patterns in price data.
4. A pure technician does not care about earnings or corporate news; he only wants to know the stock ticker and price history.

Question 6—Trend vs. Counter-Trend Trading

All of the following are advantages of trend trading over counter-trend trading, except:

1. Greater profit potential per trade
2. Lower commission expense
3. More time to make decisions
4. Lower stress level

Question 7—System vs. Discretionary Trading

System trading has all of the following advantages over discretionary trading, except:

1. Knowing in advance what profits or losses to expect over a period of time
2. Less emotional involvement in every trade
3. A greater degree of freedom
4. A method for handling the uncertainty of the markets

Question 8—Technical Toolbox

A technical trader uses a toolbox of indicators in his or her decision-making. Find the correct statement among the following:

1. Selecting the tools that give the signals you want is a sound practice.
2. The more tools, the better the toolbox.
3. "Five bullets to a clip" allows you to use only five indicators.
4. The best indicators are well known, and a trader should use them.

Question 9—New High–New Low Index

Find the incorrect statement about the New High–New Low Index:

1. NH-NL confirms uptrends by reaching new highs; it confirms downtrends by falling to new lows.
2. The signals of NH-NL are symmetrical at tops and bottoms.
3. Bearish divergences of NH-NL warn of impending market tops.
4. Downspikes of NH-NL often identify important market bottoms.

Question 10—Trading Psychology

Find the incorrect statement about trading psychology:

1. If you set your technical system just right, you need not worry about psychology.
2. The mind of a trader continually filters the incoming information.
3. Wishful thinking causes traders to "see" non-existent technical signals.
4. A bullish trader is more likely to overlook sell signals.

Question 11—Trading Discipline

Traders need discipline because the markets present an endless parade of temptations. Please identify the incorrect statement among the following:

1. People with a history of poor impulse control are likely to fail in trading.
2. AA (Alcoholics Anonymous) provides a useful model for dealing with market temptations.
3. If you have a good trading system, discipline is not really an issue.
4. Some traders have personality flaws that make them destined to fail.

Question 12—Dealing with Losses

Many traders feel ashamed of their losses. Please review the following statements and find the correct one:

1. In training, punishments are more effective than rewards.
2. If you have taken several right steps and one wrong one in making a trade, you should punish yourself for it.
3. Successful traders love the game more than the profits.
4. It does not pay to keep records of losing trades.

Question 13—Overtrading

Trading a position that is too large for one's account will lead to all of the following, except:

1. Less spontaneity and greater stiffness
2. Less calm and adaptability
3. Fear of pulling the trigger
4. A greater focus on the market

Question 14—The 2% Rule

A beginning trader with a $20,000 account decides to implement the 2% Rule of money management. He finds a stock quoted at $12.50 and decides to buy it, with a price target of $15 and a stop-loss order at $11.50. The maximum number of shares this Rule allows him to buy is close to:

1. 900
2. 400
3. 350
4. 200

Question 15—Modifying the 2% Rule

An experienced trader with a $2,000,000 account decides to modify the 2% Rule and cap his risk per trade at 0.25%. He finds a $9 stock which he plans to ride to $12, while putting his stop at $8. The maximum number of shares his Rule allows him to buy is:

1. 2,000
2. 4,500
3. 5,000
4. 12,000

Question 16—The 6% Rule

Find the statement about the 6% Rule that is correct:

1. It will protect your account from a drawdown caused by a bad trade.
2. It will protect your account from a drawdown caused by a series of bad trades.
3. When losses begin to mount, the best response is to trade more actively, to trade your way out of a hole.
4. The 6% Rule needs to be applied after putting on a trade.

Question 17—The Top Two Goals for Every Trade

What are the top two goals for every trade?

1. Make money and test a new system.
2. Face the challenge and feel the joy of victory.
3. Make money and become a better trader.
4. Test your discipline and the ability to implement a plan.

Question 18—Learning from Experience

The best way to learn from experience is:

1. To make lots of trades
2. To keep good records
3. To discuss your trades with friends
4. To review your brokerage statements

Question 19—A Record-Keeping Spreadsheet

Which of the following must be included in a basic record-keeping spreadsheet?

    A. Gross and net P&L

    B. The grade of each trade

    C. Slippage on entry and exit

    D. Source of every trade idea

1. A
2. A and B
3. A, B, and C
4. All of the above

Question 20—Trading Mistakes

Which of the following statements about trading mistakes is incorrect?

1. Intelligent people do not make mistakes.
2. Making mistakes is inevitable when you learn and explore.
3. Repeating mistakes is a sign of impulsivity.
4. Keeping a diary helps you learn from your mistakes.

Question 21—Trader's Diary

Find the correct statement about the Trader's Diary:

1. There is no need to rush documenting your entry if you plan to fill in the diary after you exit.
2. The diaries of losing trades tend to be more valuable than those of winning ones.
3. It is essential to create diary entries only for your best trades.
4. An active trader who cannot document all trades can pick and choose what trades to document.

Question 22—Diary Entry

The diary of an entry into a trade must include all of the following, except:

1. The reason for making this trade
2. The buy grade for long or sell grade for short trades
3. Charts of your trading vehicle at the time of the entry
4. The trade grade

Question 23—Trading Plan vs. Diary

Which of the following describes the difference between a Trader's Diary and a Trading Plan?

1. Contains charts in two timeframes.
2. The charts are marked up to identify buy or sell signals.
3. The document is named after the stock ticker.
4. Buy or sell grades are recorded.

Question 24—The Monitoring Screen

The window for monitoring stocks in your trading software should include all of the following, except:

1. Key market indexes
2. Your open positions
3. The stocks you consider trading
4. The stocks you have exited

Question 25—Comments on the Screen

Keeping your comments about your open positions on the screen is useful for all of the following reasons, except:

1. It reminds you how long you have been in a trade.
2. It helps you see whether you are winning or losing in an open position.
3. It helps you keep track of your profit target and stop-loss order.
4. It helps you measure your performance.

Question 26—Pinning a Chart to a Wall

"Margret's method"—pinning a chart to a wall and marking the trading signal for which you will be waiting—has all of the following advantages, except:

1. It forces you to clearly express what price or indicator action you expect.
2. It keeps you from forgetting a plan.
3. Removing the charts from the wall if your plans change helps keep your mind fresh.
4. Keeping charts on a wall ensures that you will act when the time is right.

Question 27—A Trial-Sized Order

Which of the following statements about a "Chihuahua trade"—a trial-sized order designed to draw your attention to a trading opportunity—is correct?

1. There is little difference between an electronic alert and an order for a handful of shares.
2. Chihuahua orders are good for placing stops.
3. Getting a fill on a Chihuahua order forces you to make a decision.
4. Once you have a fill on a trial-sized order, you must bring that trade up to full size.

Question 28—Grading Buys and Sells

Find the incorrect statement about grading buys or sells:

1. The closer you buy to the low of the bar, the better your grade.
2. The closer you sell to the low of the bar, the better your grade.
3. Selling above the midpoint of the bar earns a positive grade.
4. Buying in the lowest quarter of the bar earns an excellent grade.

Question 29—Grading Completed Trades

Find the correct statement about grading completed trades:

1. Money is a good measure of the quality of each trade.
2. A long-term trend trader can use channels to measure the quality of trades.
3. A trade capturing over 30% of a channel earns an "A."
4. A trade capturing less than 20% of a channel earns a "D."

Question 30—Buying

Find the incorrect statement about buying:

1. The principle of value buying is "buy low, sell high."
2. The principle of momentum buying is "buy high, sell even higher."
3. The upper channel line identifies the level of depression and the lower channel line the level of mania in the markets.
4. Momentum trading works well in runaway trends.

Question 31—Value

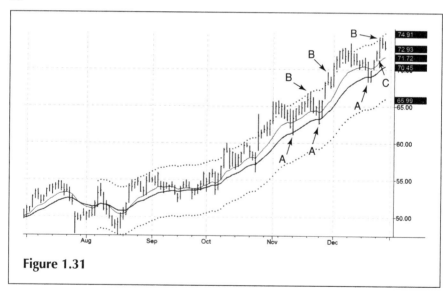

Figure 1.31

Please match the following descriptions with the letters on the chart:

1. Value zone
2. Below value—consider buying
3. Overvalued—consider selling

Question 32—The Impulse System

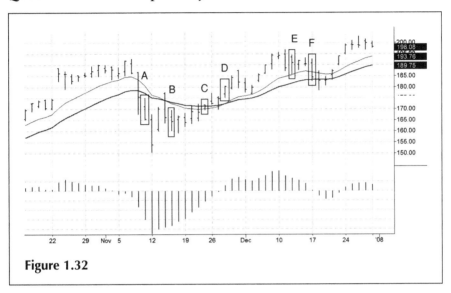

Figure 1.32

The Impulse system tracks both the inertia and the power of market moves. Some software packages allow traders to color price bars in accordance with the Impulse reading. Even on a black-and-white chart, a trader can tell what color any of the bars should be in accordance with the Impulse rules. Please match the following comments on the Impulse system with the letter bars on the chart:

1. Impulse Green—buy or stand aside; shorting not permitted
2. Impulse Red—sell short or stand aside; buying not permitted
3. Impulse Blue—no position is prohibited

Question 33—The Signals of NH-NL

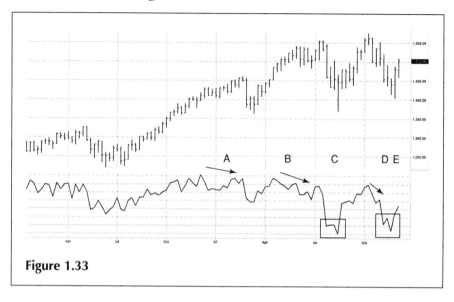

Figure 1.33

The weekly chart of New High–New Low Index (NH-NL) can help traders anticipate important turns in the stock market. Please match the following comments on NH-NL with the letters on the chart:

1. A spike identifies an unsustainable extreme and calls for a reversal.
2. A divergence identifies the weakness of the dominant crowd and calls for a reversal.

Question 34—A Trade Diary

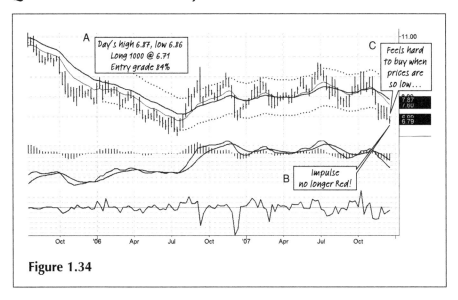

Figure 1.34

This chart comes from a Trader's Diary and illustrates an entry into a trade. Match the following with the letters on the chart:

1. A technical comment on a chart pattern that led to a trade
2. A performance rating
3. A psychological comment

Question 35—Grading a Trade

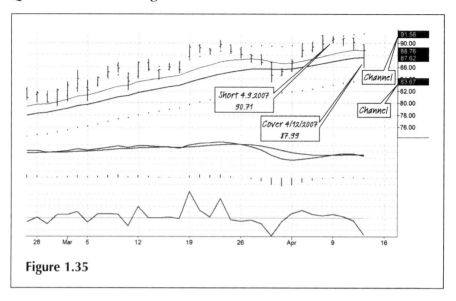

Figure 1.35

This chart shows one of the trades in which I was piggybacking a Spike pick. The weekly chart is not shown here, but you can see bearish divergences of MACD Lines and Force Index on the dailies. The question, however, is about grading this trade: in at 90.71, cover at 87.99, upper channel line at 91.56, lower channel line at 83.67. What is the trade grade?

1. Trade Grade A: Over 30% of the channel
2. Trade Grade B: 20–30% of the channel
3. Trade Grade C: 10–20% of the channel
4. Trade Grade D: Below 10% of the channel

Question 36—Value Buying vs. Momentum Buying

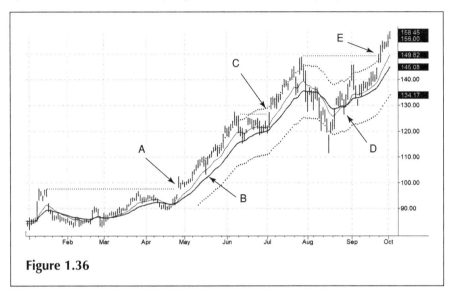

Figure 1.36

Take a look at the letters on this chart and identify which represent value buying or momentum buying zones.

1. Value buying zones
2. Momentum buying zones

HOW TO SELL

Y ou have bought a stock, and now it shows a profit. Taking your broker's statement to a store and showing it to a clerk will not buy you a bag of groceries. You need to decide when is the right time to sell your position and convert paper profits into real money. Should you sell right now, and take your money off the table? Should you let your trade ride and maybe make a lot more money later? And what if you let your trade ride but the stock reverses and your profits melt away?

Selling—the essential step of taking profits or cutting losses—must be done in a serious and businesslike manner. You need to know how to set profit targets for the stocks you buy. There is no guarantee that the stock you bought will go up, which is why you need to decide where to dump it; this decision must be made before you get into a trade. You need to know how to set protective stops.

After buying a stock, you need to bracket it with both profit-taking and stop-loss orders. You have to be prepared to adjust both with the passage of time. You also need to decide whether to sell your entire position at once or take partial profits and let the rest of the position ride.

As you work through the questions in this section, please be sure to link every answer to your own experiences as a trader. Keep referring to your diary, which you should have begun keeping by now. Selling is the longest part of this *Study Guide*, with the largest number of questions. The topic is so important that you must make sure you earn a high score, taking and retaking this test if necessary.

Answer Sheet

Questions	Max. Pts. Available	Trial 1	Trial 2	Trial 3	Trial 4	Trial 5	Trial 6
37	1						
38	1						
39	1						
40	1						
41	1						
42	1						
43	1						
44	1						
45	1						
46	1						
47	1						
48	1						
49	1						
50	1						
51	1						
52	1						
53	1						
54	1						
55	1						
56	1						
57	1						
58	1						
59	1						
60	1						
61	1						

(continuing)

Answer Sheet, *continued*

Questions	Max. Pts. Available	Trial 1	Trial 2	Trial 3	Trial 4	Trial 5	Trial 6
62	1						
63	1						
64	1						
65	1						
66	1						
67	1						
68	1						
69	1						
70	1						
71	1						
72	1						
73	1						
74	1						
75	1						
76	1						
77	1						
78	1						
79	1						
80	1						
81	1						
82	1						
83	1						
84	1						
85	1						
86	1						
Total points	50						

Question 37—A Plan for Selling

Find the incorrect statement about a written plan for selling:

1. It guarantees success.
2. It reduces stress.
3. It allows you to separate analysis from trading.
4. It makes you less prone to react to the market's zigzags.

Question 38—The Three Types of Selling

The three logical types of selling do not include which of the following?

1. Selling at a profit target above the market
2. Selling on a stop below the market
3. Selling in response to the "engine noise" of changing market conditions
4. Selling after feeling impatient about the trade

Question 39—Planning to Sell

Prior to buying a stock, serious traders ask themselves all of the following questions except:

1. How high is the stock likely to rise—what is the profit target?
2. How low does the stock have to fall to activate a protective stop?
3. What is the stock's reward-to-risk ratio?
4. Should I move my target farther away after the stock reaches it?

Question 40—Targets for Selling

Which of the following tools can help set targets for selling?

    A. Moving averages
    B. Envelopes or channels
    C. Support and resistance zones
    D. Other methods

1. A
2. A and B
3. A, B, and C
4. All of the above

Question 41—A Stock below Its Moving Average

Find two correct statements about a stock that trades below its moving average:

    A. The stock is trading below value.

    B. It is definitely headed lower.

    C. It is definitely headed higher.

    D. If the indicators are pointing higher, the first target is the moving average.

1. A and D
2. B and D
3. A and C
4. A and B

Question 42—Moving Averages as Selling Targets

Find the incorrect statement about using moving averages as selling targets:

1. Selling at a moving average works especially well on weekly charts.
2. Prices tend to oscillate above and below their moving averages.
3. It is highly desirable that the distance to the target be longer than the distance to the stop.
4. When you sell at a target, the sell grade is unimportant.

Question 43—Regrets About Selling

A trader feels intense regret after he sells at an EMA but prices continue to rise. Which of the following statements is correct?

1. Regret is good because it motivates you not to exit the next trade too soon.
2. A strong feeling of regret about exiting early can lead to overstaying the next trade.
3. If your analysis is good, you should know not to sell early.
4. Leaving money on the table is a sign of a poor trader.

Question 44—The Timing of a Sale Near the EMA

What is the best time to use an EMA as a target for a rally?

1. When prices rally from bear market lows
2. In the midst of an ongoing uptrend
3. When prices are boiling near their historic highs
4. All of the above

Question 45—Channels as Price Targets

Find the correct statement about using channels as price targets:

1. A powerful upmove on the weekly charts is the best time to target channels on the dailies.
2. Uptrends rarely show an orderly pattern of tops and bottoms.
3. The best time to go long in an uptrend is when prices hit the upper channel.
4. It does not pay to sell at a channel because prices may rally higher.

Question 46—Measuring Performance Using Channels

Measuring the percentage of a channel height captured in a trade can help a swing trader:

    A. Focus on points rather than dollars.

    B. Provide a yardstick for measuring one's progress.

    C. Set a realistic profit target.

1. A
2. A and B
3. All of the above

Question 47—Selling Targets

Please find statements that match among the following two pairs of statements:

    A. The first target for selling into a rally off the lows

    B. The first target for selling in an ongoing uptrend

1. At or below value, as defined by moving averages
2. Near the overvalued zone, as defined by the upper channel line

Question 48—Reaching for a Greater Profit

Always reaching out for a greater profit makes a trader:

    A. More relaxed

    B. More stressed

    C. More successful

    D. More hyperactive

1. A and B
2. A and C
3. B and D
4. B and C

Question 49—The Top of a Rally

Find the correct statement about the top tick of a rally:

1. Forecasting it will provide a reasonable target for selling.
2. It can be forecast with a good degree of consistency.
3. Trying to sell at the top tick tends to be a very expensive undertaking.
4. If one can sell consistently at the absolute top, one can also sell short there.

Question 50—Prices above the Upper Channel Line

Assume that prices have rallied above the upper channel line; find the correct statement among the following:

1. A trader must immediately take profits.
2. When prices close above the upper channel line for two days in a row, a trader must take profits.
3. When prices close above the upper channel line, it means the rally will continue.
4. When prices close above the upper channel line but then fail to reach a new high, the trader should consider selling that day.

Question 51—Setting Profit Targets

Find the correct statement about setting profit targets:

1. Let the trade run as far as it will without worrying about targets.
2. There is a perfect profit target for any market.
3. The longer your time horizon, the farther away the profit target.
4. A moving average provides the best profit target for any trade.

Question 52—Support and Resistance Zones as Targets

Support and resistance zones provide attractive price targets for long-term trades for all of the following reasons, except:

1. Congestion zones show where the masses of market participants are prepared to buy or sell.
2. A trading range represents a general consensus of value among huge masses of traders.
3. The duration of trading ranges tends to be longer than that of price trends.
4. A trend always stops at the edge of a trading range.

Question 53—A Protective Stop

Using a protective stop makes sense for all of the following reasons, except:

1. It is a reality check, reminding you that prices can move against you.
2. It works against the ownership effect, when people fall in love with their stocks.
3. It reduces the emotional stress of making decisions in open trades.
4. It puts an absolute limit on the amount of dollars you can lose in any given trade.

Question 54—Breaking through Resistance

If a stock rises to its resistance level, stays there, and then rallies and closes above that level, it gives us a signal to:

    A. Go long immediately.
    B. Get ready to sell short if the stock sinks back into its resistance zone.
    C. Sell short immediately.
    D. Get ready to buy if the stock declines towards its resistance zone.

1. A or D
2. A or B
3. B or C
4. C or D

Question 55—A Trade without a Stop

A trade without a stop is:

1. Permitted only for experienced traders
2. A gamble
3. A way to be more flexible
4. A realistic approach to trading

Question 56—Changing Stops

Which of the following are allowed during a trade?

    A. Raising stops on longs
    B. Raising stops on shorts
    C. Lowering stops on shorts
    D. Lowering stops on longs

1. A and B
2. B and C
3. A and C
4. C and D

Question 57—Re-Entering a Trade

Buying a stock, getting stopped out, and then re-entering the trade by buying that stock back is:

1. A common tactic among professionals
2. Throwing good money after bad
3. A sign of stubbornness
4. A waste of time and money that could be spent on better opportunities

Question 58—Deciding Where to Set a Stop

The single most important question in setting a stop is:

1. What is the volatility of the market you are trading?
2. How much money are you prepared to risk?
3. What is your profit target?
4. How many shares are you planning to buy?

Question 59—The Impact of the Last Trade

What impact should the size of your latest profit or loss have on your plans for the next trade?

1. Trade a bigger size after a profitable trade.
2. Trade a smaller size after an unprofitable trade.
3. Trade a bigger size after an unprofitable trade.
4. None of the above

Question 60—"The Iron Triangle"

Please match the components of "The Iron Triangle" of risk control with their descriptions:

  A. Money management
  B. Stop placement
  C. Position sizing

1. Set it on the basis of chart analysis.
2. Decide how much money you will risk in this trade.
3. Divide one of the three factors by another.

Question 61—A Limit Order

A limit order is preferable to a market order for all of the following reasons except:

1. It prevents slippage.
2. It guarantees execution.
3. It works best for entering trades.
4. It is useful for taking profits at target levels.

Question 62—Soft Stops

Which of the following statements about soft stops is correct?

1. They are very useful for system traders.
2. They offer a good way to get started in the markets.
3. They help avoid whipsaws.
4. They are easier to set than hard stops.

Question 63—A Stop One Tick below the Latest Low

Putting a protective stop on a long position one tick below the latest low is problematic for all of the following reasons, except:

1. Even a small sell order thrown at the market near the lows can briefly push it below the latest low.
2. A bullish pattern occurs when a market takes out its previous low by a small margin and reverses.
3. Professionals like to fade (trade against) breakouts.
4. Once the low is taken out, prices are likely to decline much lower.

Question 64—A Stop at the Level of the Previous Low

Placing a stop exactly at the level of the previous low can be good for all of the following reasons, except:

1. A downtrend often slows down as it approaches the level of the previous low.
2. If the stock declines to its previous low, it is likely to go even lower.
3. Stocks often accelerate immediately after taking the previous low.
4. Slippage tends to be higher when the stop is at the level of the previous low rather than one tick below that low.

Question 65—A Stop That Is "Tighter by a Day"

Find the correct statement about a stop that is "tighter by a day" ("Nic's Stop"):

1. Examine the bars that bracket a recent low and place your stop a little below the lower of those two bars.
2. Using a tight stop is not suitable for short-term trading.
3. This method is especially useful for long-term position trades.
4. A tight stop like this one eliminates slippage.

Question 66—Trade Duration

The outcome of a trade depends in part on the duration of that trade. Find the incorrect statement about the impact of trade duration:

1. Longer-term trades give you the luxury of time to think and make decisions.
2. If a day-trader stops to think, he loses.
3. The more time a stock has, the farther it can move.
4. Long-term position trades provide the best learning experience.

Question 67—Wider Stops

Find the correct statement about using wider stops:

1. A major uptrend is less volatile than a minor one.
2. The wider the stop, the greater the risk of a whipsaw.
3. A stop belongs outside of the zone of the normal chop of prices.
4. The wider the stop, the larger position you can carry.

Question 68—Moving Stops

Which of the following statements about moving stops is incorrect?

1. You may move stops only in the direction of the trade but never against it.
2. When you switch to a trailing stop after the prices reach their target you increase your risk.
3. When prices hang just above your stop, it makes sense to lower it to reduce the risk of a whipsaw.
4. When prices move in your favor, it makes sense to raise your stop to protect a part of your paper profit.

Question 69—The SafeZone Stops

Find the correct statement about the SafeZone stop:

1. It acts as a filter that suppresses the signal of the trend.
2. Noise is any part of today's range that protrudes outside of the previous day's range.
3. SafeZone tracks Average Upside Penetration in uptrends and Average Downside Penetration in downtrends.
4. SafeZone works best during trends and worst during trading ranges.

Question 70—Trading with the SafeZone

Which of the following statements about SafeZone stops is incorrect?

1. SafeZone is a mechanical trading system.
2. You have to establish the lookback period for the SafeZone.
3. You need to choose the coefficient by which to multiply the normal noise to obtain the SafeZone stop.
4. Usually, a coefficient between two and three provides a margin of safety.

Question 71—The Volatility-Drop Method

Which of the following statements about the Volatility-Drop method is incorrect?

1. A Volatility-Drop ensures getting greater profit from every trade.
2. This methods allows a trader to start out with a modest target, but reach out for more while in the trade.
3. Using a Volatility-Drop stop involves risking some of the paper profit.
4. Using this method helps automate profit-taking decisions.

Question 72—"Engine Noise" in the Markets

Selling "engine noise" refers to selling when:

1. Your target is reached.
2. Your stop is hit.
3. You want to take partial profits.
4. You do not like how the market is acting.

Question 73—Selling "Engine Noise"

Which statement about selling "engine noise" is incorrect?

1. A system trader may not sell "engine noise."
2. A discretionary trader may exit the market sooner or later than planned.
3. Selling "engine noise" is especially well suited for beginning traders.
4. Selling "engine noise" carries a risk of cutting profits.

Question 74—Not Liking Market's Action

You are holding a long position but do not like the toppy signals of indicators. Which statement about the courses of action open to you is incorrect?

1. If you are a system trader, you must hold your position as planned.
2. If you are a discretionary trader, you may sell your position.
3. If you are a system trader, you may switch to a different system that allows an earlier exit.
4. If you are a discretionary trader, you may take partial profits but retain the core position.

Question 75—Earnings Reports

Which statement about the impact of earnings reports is incorrect?

1. Prices are largely driven by the anticipation of future earnings.
2. An earnings report never changes a long-term stock trend.
3. Earnings reports rarely come as a surprise to professional watchers.
4. Insider trading is usually linked to the way a company is managed.

Question 76—The Market "Rings a Bell"

The market "rings a bell" when:

1. It makes a multiyear high.
2. It falls to a multiyear low.
3. An event occurs far outside the norm for this market.
4. The market flashes a signal anyone can recognize.

Question 77—Trading with the New High–New Low Index

Which statement about the New High–New Low Index (NH-NL) is incorrect?

1. When NH-NL is above zero it shows that bulls are stronger than bears.
2. New Highs are the leaders in weakness and New Lows are the leaders in strength.
3. Bearish divergences are commonly seen near the ends of bull markets.
4. A severe downspike of weekly NH-NL usually signals a market bottom.

Question 78—A Decision-Making Tree vs. a Trading System

The key difference between a decision-making tree and a trading system is that only one of them includes:

1. The rules for entering a trade
2. The rules for exiting a trade
3. The permission to bend your exit rules
4. The parameters for trade sizing

Question 79—A Decision-Making Tree

Which of the following questions does not belong in a decision-making tree:

1. Is this a short-term or a long-term trade?
2. Where will you place your stop?
3. What kind of "engine noise" will you listen to while in a trade?
4. What kind of record-keeping will you perform for a trade?

Question 80—Value Buying and Selling Targets

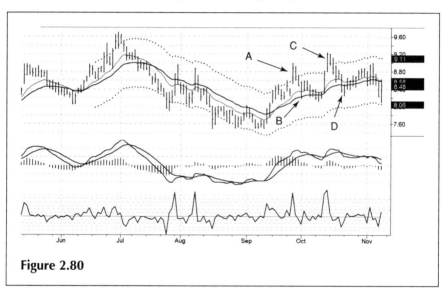

Figure 2.80

Please identify value buying zones and selling targets among the letter points on this chart:

1. Value buying zones
2. Selling targets in overvalued zones

Question 81—Support, Resistance, and Targets

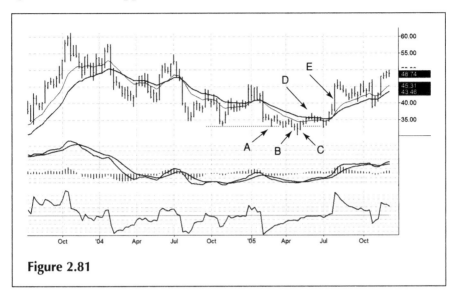

Figure 2.81

Please match the following descriptions with the letters on the chart:

1. Line of support broken
2. Prices close above support, giving a signal to buy
3. Support established
4. Second selling target at the upper channel line
5. First selling target at the EMA

Question 82—Multiple Targets

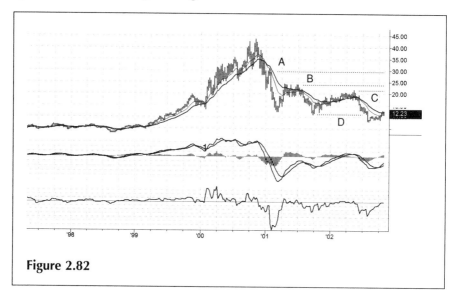

Figure 2.82

Please match the following descriptions with the letters on this monthly chart:

1. The minimal price target
2. Support
3. The bull market target

Question 83—Holding, Adding, or Profit-Taking

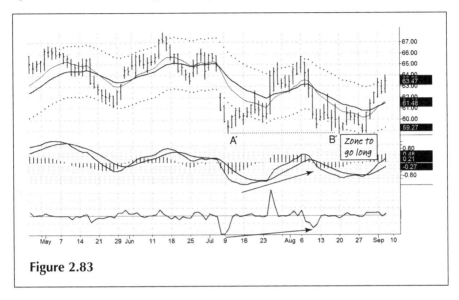

Figure 2.83

At point **A'** the stock declined to 58.78. At point **B'** it fell to 58.71 but recoiled from its new low. This false downside breakout was accompanied by bullish divergences in several indicators. If a trader went long with a target near the upper channel line, which of the following actions are legitimate at the right edge of this chart?

 A. Sell and take profits.

 B. Sell half, hold half.

 C. Continue to hold, tighten the stop.

 D. Add to the winning position.

1. A

2. A or B

3. A, B, or C

4. All of the above

Question 84—Handling a Profitable Trade

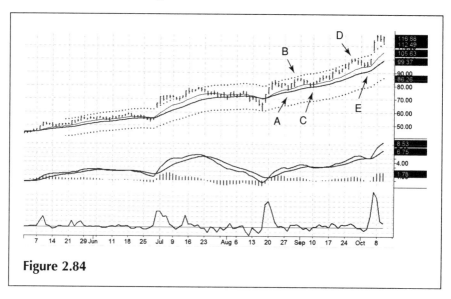

Figure 2.84

A trader recognizes an uptrend and starts buying the stock near value, selling near the upper channel line. He goes long at point **A** and sells at **B**, long at point **C** and sells at **D**, long again at point **E**. When prices gap above the upper channel line he decides to hold for a greater gain. What is the wise course of action at the right edge of this chart?

1. Sell and take profits.
2. Sell half the position.
3. Hold the position.
4. Add to the position.

Question 85—Placing a Stop

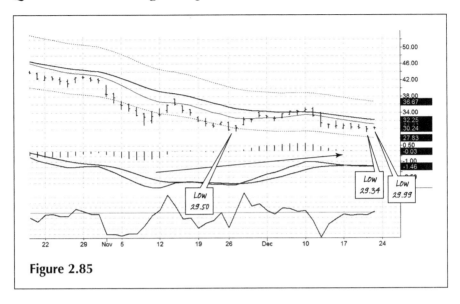

Figure 2.85

A trader recognizes a bullish divergence accompanied by a false down-side breakout. He decides to go long, but needs to place a stop. At which of the following levels would he be advised to place it?

1. 29.49
2. 29.33
3. 29.34
4. 29.98
5. 28.99

Question 86—The Decision at the Right Edge of the Chart

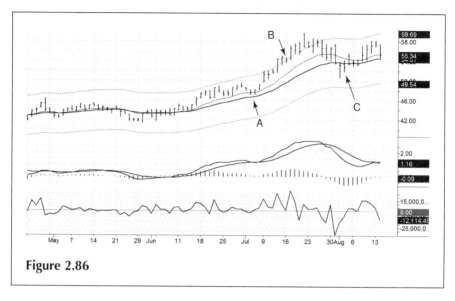

Figure 2.86

A trader recognizes an uptrend and goes long at point **A**. He sells at point **B**, after prices blow out of their channel but then fail to make a new high. He buys again at point **C**, after prices decline below value and stop making new lows. What would be the reasonable course of action at the right edge of this chart?

1. Continue to hold.
2. Add to long position.
3. Sell.

How to Sell Short

Markets rise and fall, but the vast majority of traders and investors miss half of the action. They try to profit only from going long. Every beginner buys something, but it takes an experienced trader to recognize an overvalued market and sell it short.

Shorting—profiting from market declines—is one of the favorite games of market professionals. They account for the bulk of shorting in most markets. Whenever you see a situation in which the mass of amateurs is crowding one side of an issue, while the more experienced and better capitalized professionals are on the opposite side, ask yourself—which side is more likely to win? That is the side of the market you want to be on.

It pays to run your trading account like a hedge fund, with some long and some short positions at any given time, shifting their balance as your view of the market changes. Being comfortable with selling short allows you to wrestle with the market while standing on both feet. This is a much better stance for a battle than standing on just one foot, only going long. The ability to go short when circumstances warrant is one of the key assets of a serious trader.

Selling short has its own challenges and peculiarities which you must master. This chapter will test your knowledge of the basic concepts of shorting tops and downtrends. It will quiz you on the pluses and minuses of shorting, on short interest, and on selecting stocks for shorting. It will also ask you about shorting non-equity instruments.

Answer Sheet

Questions	Max. Pts. Available	Trial 1	Trial 2	Trial 3	Trial 4	Trial 5	Trial 6
87	1						
88	1						
89	1						
90	1						
91	1						
92	1						
93	1						
94	1						
95	1						
96	1						
97	1						
98	1						
99	1						
100	1						
101	1						
102	1						
103	1						
104	1						
105	1						
106	1						
107	1						
108	1						
109	1						
110	1						

(continuing)

Answer Sheet, *continued*

Questions	Max. Pts. Available	Trial 1	Trial 2	Trial 3	Trial 4	Trial 5	Trial 6
111	1						
112	1						
113	1						
114	1						
115	1						
Total points	29						

Question 87—Shorting a Stock

Selling a stock short means:

1. Selling an overvalued stock from your portfolio
2. Selling a borrowed stock
3. Selling a stock in a severe downtrend
4. Selling a stock you expect to be delisted

Question 88—Risk Factors in Shorting

The major risk factors in selling short include all of the following, except:

1. A stock might rally.
2. A stock might issue a dividend.
3. A stock might be called back by the owner.
4. A stock might crash.

Question 89—The Impact of Shorting

People who sell stocks short help create a more orderly market through all of the following, except:

1. Dampening price increases
2. Cushioning price declines
3. Increasing price swings
4. Dampening volatility

Question 90—Short vs. Long

The main advantage of shorting over buying is that:

1. Tops are easier to recognize than bottoms.
2. Stocks fall faster than they rise.
3. It is easier to sell into a rally than buy into a decline.
4. Stocks rise faster than they fall.

Question 91—Disadvantages of Shorting

The greatest disadvantage in shorting stocks is that the stock market:

1. Keeps fluctuating
2. Has relatively slow rises and fast declines
3. Rises over time
4. Has an uptick rule

Question 92—Learning to Sell Short

Which statement about learning to sell short is incorrect?

1. Find a stock you'd hate to own.
2. Trade a large size to make the experience worthwhile.
3. Avoid shorting stocks making new highs.
4. Look for expensive stocks.

Question 93—Shorting vs. Buying

Find the correct statement among the following comparisons of buying and shorting:

1. Tops take longer to form than bottoms.
2. Stock bottoms are built on hope and greed.
3. Precise timing is more important in buying than shorting.
4. Fear is the dominant emotion of stock tops.

Question 94—Shorting Stock Market Tops

Which statement about shorting stock market tops is incorrect?

1. Stops need to be placed relatively farther away, due to high volatility.
2. Wider stops require larger positions.
3. There is nothing wrong with trying to re-enter a trade after getting stopped out.
4. Trading positions smaller than the maximum allowed by money management rules increase holding power.

Question 95—Shorting in Downtrends

Find the correct statement regarding shorting in downtrends:

1. Shorting in the middle of a channel means shorting above value.
2. Covering near the lower channel line means buying below value.
3. There is only one good shorting opportunity within a channel.
4. Grading your trades by the percentage of a channel does not work for shorting.

Question 96—The Tactics of Shorting Downtrends

Find the incorrect statement about shorting in downtrends:

1. Make a strategic decision on the weekly chart, make tactical plans on the daily.
2. Shorting within a channel lowers both the risk and the potential rewards.
3. Shorting within a channel increases the risk of a whipsaw.
4. A single short within a channel will not catch a major move.

Question 97—Shorting the Fundamentals

Find the correct statement about shorting on the basis of fundamental information:

1. A fundamental analyst can cover more markets than a technician.
2. One can use technical studies as an idea generator and fundamentals as a trigger.
3. Fundamental information overrides technical factors.
4. The most powerful situation exists when the fundamentals suggest a trade and technical factors confirm that signal.

Question 98—Looking for Shorting Candidates

Which of the following is not a valid method of looking for shorting candidates?

1. Looking at the weakest stock industry groups
2. Listening to rumors and tips, then checking them using your analytic method
3. Looking for the weakest stocks among the Nasdaq 100
4. Selling short stocks that are being upgraded by major analysts

Question 99—The Short Interest Ratio

The Short Interest Ratio reflects the intensity of shorting by measuring:

1. The number of shares held short by the bears relative to the "free float."
2. The number of stocks shorted by a trader relative to the number of shares he bought.
3. The number of traders holding shorts relative to the number of traders holding longs.
4. The number of traders whose accounts are set up for shorting relative to the total number of traders.

Question 100—Trading the Short Interest Ratio

Tracking the Short Interest Ratio can help a trader in all of the following ways, except:

1. A rising Short Interest Ratio confirms a downtrend.
2. A Short Interest Ratio over 20% warns that the stock is liable to have a sharp rally.
3. A Short Interest Ratio under 10% means that shorting is relatively safe.
4. A falling Short Interest Ratio calls for a break in the stock.

Question 101—Markets Need Shorting

Which of the following markets could exist without shorting?

1. Stocks
2. Futures
3. Options
4. Forex

Question 102—Who Shorts Futures

Most shorts in the futures markets are being held by:

1. Public speculators
2. Commercials or hedgers
3. CFTC
4. Hedge funds

Question 103—Shorting Futures

Find the incorrect statement about shorting futures:

1. A seller enters into a binding contract for future delivery.
2. The floor for a commodity price is defined by its cost of production.
3. Insider trading is illegal in futures.
4. The ceiling for a commodity price is defined by the cost of substitution.

Question 104—Long Rallies and Sharp Breaks

What is the main factor that makes many commodities prone to steady increases, punctuated by sharp declines?

1. Carrying charges
2. Manipulation
3. Seasonal factors
4. Cost of substitution

Question 105—Writing Options

What is the main reason that options writing is much more profitable than buying?

1. The time value of options
2. Most buyers are undercapitalized.
3. Options move differently than stocks.
4. Most buyers are beginners.

Question 106—Writing Covered Options

What is the main disadvantage of writing covered options?

1. If the stock stays flat, you will have no capital gain in it.
2. If the stock falls, your long position will lose value.
3. If the stock rises above the exercise price, it will be called away.
4. Covered writing requires large capital.

Question 107—Naked vs. Covered Writing

What is the main difference between naked and covered options writing?

1. Trade duration
2. How the trades are backed
3. Trade size
4. The analytic techniques

Question 108—The Demands of Naked Writing

The greatest demand that naked writing of options places on traders is:

1. Cash
2. Trading ideas
3. Discipline
4. Timing

Question 109—Brokers Against Traders

In the following list of venues for trading forex, where does a broker's profit usually depend on a trader's loss?

1. The interbank market
2. Currency futures
3. Holding foreign cash
4. Forex trading houses

Question 110—Forex Market

Which of the following does not apply to the forex market?

1. It is one of the most trending markets on a long-term basis.
2. It is largely driven by the fundamentals of government policies.
3. It is easy to plan and enter trades in forex.
4. It trades essentially 24/7.

Question 111—Learning to Become a Better Trader

The most important factor in learning to become a better trader is:

1. Researching the market
2. Keeping good records
3. Finessing your entry and exit techniques
4. Luck

Question 112—Trading Signals of Force Index

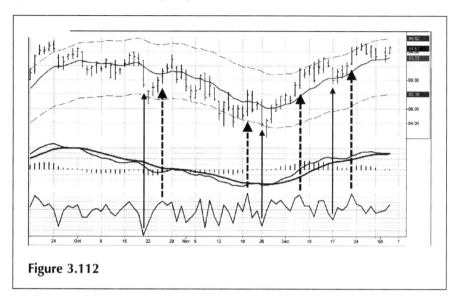

Figure 3.112

On the chart above, you can see that the downspikes of Force Index (marked by solid arrows) tend to be followed by price bottoms the following day. The chart also shows that the upspikes of Force Index (marked by dashed arrows) tend to be followed by the continuation of the uptrend rather than a top. These differences indicate that:

1. This indicator works only in downtrends.
2. This indicator works only in uptrends.
3. Uptrends and downtrends are not symmetrical and have to be traded differently.
4. One can base a trade on a single indicator in a bear market.

Question 113—False Breakouts and Divergences

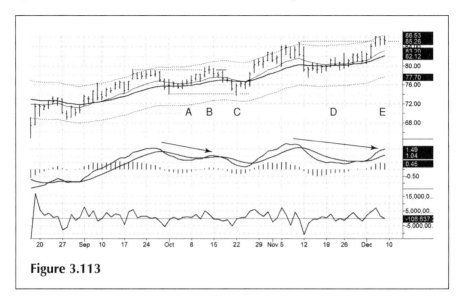

Figure 3.113

Please match the letters on the chart to the following descriptions:

1. False breakouts
2. Divergences

Question 114—Shorting and Covering Signals

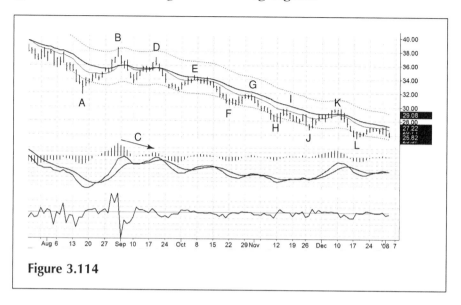

Figure 3.114

Please match the letters on the chart to the following descriptions:

1. Pullbacks to value
2. Undervalued zone
3. Kangaroo tails
4. Divergences

Question 115—Shorting Tactics

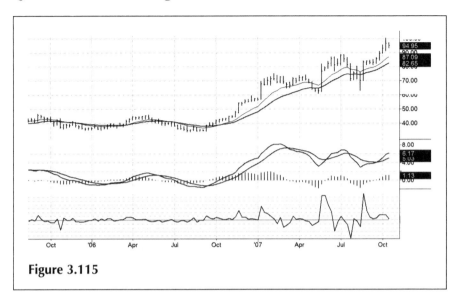

Figure 3.115

Please select the tactic to follow for the next few weeks at the right edge of the chart:

1. The trend is up—buy here, near $94.95.
2. The trend is up—buy on a breakout above the recent peak of $100.50.
3. The Impulse system turned Blue with the downtick of MACD—sell short, with the target of $87, near the fast EMA.
4. The Impulse system turned Blue—sell short with a target of $81, near the slow EMA.

ANSWERS AND RATING SCALES

How to Buy, Manage Risk, & Keep Records

Question 1—The Stress of Holding a Position

Having bought a stock, most people find themselves in the least stressful position if that stock:

1. Rises slightly
2. Skyrockets
3. Declines slightly
4. Collapses

Answer: 3

Sitting back and doing nothing feels easy; thinking and making decisions is hard. While a collapse in your stock feels painful, the rise is also stressful because it forces you to think about your exit strategy, targets, stops, and so on. Most people are surprisingly comfortable sitting with a slightly losing position and hoping for better.

Question 2—Your Trading Edge

Your trading edge can come from:

1. Fundamental analysis
2. Technical studies
3. Discipline
4. All of the above

Answer: 4

An edge is a method of discovering opportunities and placing orders that gives a trader an advantage over the majority of competitors. A trader with either a technical or a fundamental edge still needs discipline to implement trading signals.

Question 3—The Three Great Divides

The three great divides in trading include all of the following, except:

1. Technical vs. fundamental research
2. Trend vs. counter-trend trading
3. Relying on TV news vs. an advisory service
4. Discretionary vs. systematic trading

   Answer: 3

A serious trader needs to specialize by choosing those areas of research and trading that appeal to him. Choosing between technical or fundamental analysis, trend or counter-trend trading, and discretionary or systematic trading are all serious choices. Your selections depend to a great degree on your temperament and personality. A successful trader is an independent person. Hooking yourself up to the feeding line of either TV news or an advisory service is really no choice at all, since there is so little difference between them.

Question 4—Price and Value

Find the incorrect statement about the relationship between price and value:

1. Values change slowly, prices change fast.
2. Studying earnings reports and industry trends allows you to discover value.
3. Moving averages help define the value zone by tracking public consensus.
4. Price equals value at any given moment.

   Answer: 4

Prices are easily seen while you need to look for values. Prices can change quickly in response to the mood of the masses, while values change slowly. Each price is a momentary consensus of value, but that consensus keeps changing, overshooting value on the way up or down. A simple tool, such as a pair of moving averages, helps you get a general idea of where the value is and which way it is moving—and allows you to trade accordingly.

Question 5—Fundamental and Technical Analysis

Which of the following statements about fundamental and technical analysis is incorrect?

1. A fundamentalist calculates the value of the business that issued a stock.
2. Having precise information about the fundamentals tells you exactly which way a stock is going to go.
3. A technician looks for repetitive patterns in price data.
4. A pure technician does not care about earnings or corporate news; he only wants to know the stock ticker and price history.

Answer: 2

Having precise information about the fundamentals does *not* forecast exactly which way a stock is going to go. The problem with fundamental analysis is that values change slowly but prices fluctuate fast. In the short run, prices can even move against the fundamentals. Whether you are primarily a fundamentalist or a technician, you want to know how the other side lives and thinks. Having both a fundamental and a technical view of a stock provides a deeper understanding of its trends and reversals.

Question 6—Trend vs. Counter-Trend Trading

All of the following are advantages of trend trading over counter-trend trading, except:

1. Greater profit potential per trade
2. Lower commission expense
3. More time to make decisions
4. Lower stress level

Answer: 4

Trend trades last longer than counter-trend moves, giving you more time to make trade-related decisions. They promise greater profits by covering longer distances. Commissions are lower in trend-following trades than in active swing trading. Still, it would be incorrect to expect a lower stress level. Riding a trend is like riding a bucking horse that tries to shake you off. Holding on to a trend-following trade requires a great deal of patience and self-assurance—a lot of mental work.

Question 7—System vs. Discretionary Trading

System trading has all of the following advantages over discretionary trading, except:

1. Knowing in advance what profits or losses to expect over a period of time
2. Less emotional involvement in every trade
3. A greater degree of freedom
4. A method for handling the uncertainty of the markets

Answer: 3

System traders who have done a lot of backtesting can have a fairly high level of confidence knowing what profits or losses to expect down the road. If they have the discipline to follow all the signals of their system, they will lower their stress level, insulating themselves to a degree from uncertainty in the markets. What they give up is the freedom to make decisions as market conditions change and create new threats or opportunities.

Question 8—Technical Toolbox

A technical trader uses a toolbox of indicators in his or her decision-making. Find the correct statement among the following:

1. Selecting the tools that give the signals you want is a sound practice.
2. The more tools, the better the toolbox.
3. "Five bullets to a clip" allows you to use only five indicators.
4. The best indicators are well known, and a trader should use them.

Answer: 3

A typical beginners' mistake is to overstuff their toolbox; they also tend to use different tools at different times to confirm their preconceptions. It is much better to limit yourself to a small number of well-tested tools. Which tools are used, however, may very well vary among different traders.

Question 9—New High–New Low Index

Find the incorrect statement about the New High–New Low Index:

1. NH-NL confirms uptrends by reaching new highs; it confirms downtrends by falling to new lows.
2. The signals of NH-NL are symmetrical at tops and bottoms.
3. Bearish divergences of NH-NL warn of impending market tops.
4. Downspikes of NH-NL often identify important market bottoms.

Answer: 2

NH-NL may be the best leading indicator of the stock market, but it behaves differently at tops and bottoms. The emotions of the market crowds are different in those areas. Tops are formed by greed which tends to last a lot longer than fear, the dominant emotion at market bottoms. This is why the best signals of the tops are longer-lasting divergences, while the best signals of the bottoms are brief and violent downspikes.

Question 10—Trading Psychology

Find the incorrect statement about trading psychology:

1. If you set your technical system just right, you need not worry about psychology.
2. The mind of a trader continually filters the incoming information.
3. Wishful thinking causes traders to "see" non-existent technical signals.
4. A bullish trader is more likely to overlook sell signals.

Answer: 1

The sheer volume of information available to us is so immense that no human can process everything. Our eyes, ears, and brains filter out much of incoming data. We become consciously aware of only a small part of market information. Our wishes, hopes, and fears filter out much of the rest. Trading systems have their advantages, but it would be a humanly impossible task to switch off our personal psychology, in the markets or anywhere else.

Question 11—Trading Discipline

Traders need discipline because the markets present an endless parade of temptations. Please identify the incorrect statement among the following:

1. People with a history of poor impulse control are likely to fail in trading.
2. AA (Alcoholics Anonymous) provides a useful model for dealing with market temptations.
3. If you have a good trading system, discipline is not really an issue.
4. Some traders have personality flaws that make them destined to fail.

Answer: 3

The seemingly easy riches that glitter on every screen seduce many traders to plunge into the market without considering its very real dangers. You need discipline to set up and follow your decision-making tree. You must decide when to step in and when to stay out. People who cannot resist temptation are likely to do poorly in trading, no matter how smart they are.

Question 12—Dealing with Losses

Many traders feel ashamed of their losses. Please review the following statements and find the correct one:

1. In training, punishments are more effective than rewards.
2. If you have taken several right steps and one wrong one in making a trade, you should punish yourself for it.
3. Successful traders love the game more than the profits.
4. It does not pay to keep records of losing trades.

Answer: 3

Rewarding people tends to improve their performance much more than punishments. It pays to be kind to yourself while learning how to trade. Give yourself sufficient time to learn; celebrate even partial successes. Keep good notes of all your trades—you will probably learn more from losses than from wins. Trade a small size, so that you can focus on the game and not on the money. You can always increase your trading size later, after you become more knowledgeable and secure.

Question 13—Overtrading

Trading a position that is too large for one's account will lead to all of the following, except:

1. Less spontaneity and greater stiffness
2. Less calm and adaptability
3. Fear of pulling the trigger
4. A greater focus on the market

Answer: 4

When stakes become dangerously high, people become stiff with tension and are afraid to pull the trigger. The spontaneity and ease of adjustment deteriorate, and performance goes down accordingly. A trader whose position is too large for his account is not focusing on the market. He is focusing on the money. The feeling of tension clouds his mind, preventing him from reading the market's signals. One of the key goals of money management is to put your mind at ease by setting realistic position limits and providing a safety net for your account.

Question 14—The 2% Rule

A beginning trader with a $20,000 account decides to implement the 2% Rule of money management. He finds a stock quoted at $12.50 and decides to buy it, with a price target of $15 and a stop-loss order at $11.50. The maximum number of shares this Rule allows him to buy is close to:

1. 900
2. 400
3. 350
4. 200

Answer: 3

A trader who decides to risk no more than 2% of his account in any given trade may risk the maximum of $400 in a $20,000 account. Of course, he is free to risk less. Buying a stock at $12.50 and putting a stop at $11.50 means risking $1 per share. In a perfect world, this rule would have allowed him to buy 400 shares, but in reality this trader will have to pay a commission when he buys and again when he sells;

he can also expect to be hit with slippage. This is why 350 shares is the correct answer. He may buy even fewer shares but he may not buy a greater number.

Question 15—Modifying the 2% Rule

An experienced trader with a $2,000,000 account decides to modify the 2% Rule and cap his risk per trade at 0.25%. He finds a $9 stock which he plans to ride to $12, while putting his stop at $8. The maximum number of shares his Rule allows him to buy is:

1. 2,000
2. 4,500
3. 5,000
4. 12,000

Answer: 2

As a rule, the larger the account, the lower the percentage a trader will risk on any single trade. The maximum for him is the same as for everyone else—2%; still, he may go up to that absolute limit only when he sees an exceptional opportunity. At other times he is likely to limit his risk to well below 1%. For a trader with a $2,000,000 account, a quarter percent comes to $5,000—quite a bit to bet on a single trade. Risking $1 per share means a theoretical maximum size of 5,000 shares. In practice, the size has to be reduced, to pay commissions and to cover possible slippage.

Question 16—The 6% Rule

Find the statement about the 6% Rule that is correct:

1. It will protect your account from a drawdown caused by a bad trade.
2. It will protect your account from a drawdown caused by a series of bad trades.
3. When losses begin to mount, the best response is to trade more actively, to trade your way out of a hole.
4. The 6% Rule needs to be applied after putting on a trade.

Answer: 2

The 2% Rule is designed to limit risk on any single trade, but the 6% Rule will protect you from the damage caused by a series of bad trades. The 6% Rule will force you to step back when losses begin to mount; this is the opposite of what most traders do, as they dig themselves a deeper hole by frantic trading. The time to apply the 6% Rule is before you enter a trade, not after. It helps you to see whether you can afford the risk of an additional trade.

Question 17—The Top Two Goals for Every Trade

What are the top two goals for every trade?

1. Make money and test a new system.
2. Face the challenge and feel the joy of victory.
3. Make money and become a better trader.
4. Test your discipline and the ability to implement a plan.

   Answer: 3

The main reason to trade is to make money, but there is a fair bit of randomness in the markets, and not every trade can be profitable. On the other hand, becoming a better trader is a very reachable goal for every trade. Whether you win or lose, you must become a better trader at the conclusion of each trade. You must keep learning both from your winning and losing trades. Testing your discipline and the ability to implement a plan are key components of learning to become a better trader.

Question 18—Learning from Experience

The best way to learn from experience is:

1. To make lots of trades
2. To keep good records
3. To discuss your trades with friends
4. To review your brokerage statements

   Answer: 2

A human mind has a limited capacity to remember. Keeping good records allows you to transform fleeting experiences into solid memories. Using your notes as your "extracranial memory" allows you to re-examine your experiences and grow into a better trader. A trader who uses money management rules to protect his equity and who keeps good records to learn from his experience is on the road to success.

Question 19—A Record-Keeping Spreadsheet

Which of the following must be included in a basic record-keeping spreadsheet?

  A. Gross and net P&L

  B. The grade of each trade

  C. Slippage on entry and exit

  D. Source of every trade idea

1. A
2. A and B
3. A, B, and C
4. All of above

  Answer: 4

The purpose of keeping a trader's spreadsheet is to record hard facts about your trading. In addition to such basic data as entry and exit prices, you need to calculate slippage, track the quality of your sources, and grade your performance for every entry and exit, as well as for each trade.

Question 20—Trading Mistakes

Which of the following statements about trading mistakes is incorrect?

1. Intelligent people do not make mistakes.
2. Making mistakes is inevitable when you learn and explore.
3. Repeating mistakes is a sign of impulsivity.
4. Keeping a diary helps you learn from your mistakes.

  Answer: 1

Mistakes are part and parcel of learning and exploring—which is why intelligent people often make them. There is nothing wrong with making a mistake—the problem is repeating the same mistake. Keeping a diary helps you avoid this problem.

Question 21—Trader's Diary

Find the correct statement about the Trader's Diary:

1. There is no need to rush documenting your entry if you plan to fill in the diary after you exit.
2. The diaries of losing trades tend to be more valuable than those of winning ones.
3. It is essential to create diary entries only for your best trades.
4. An active trader who cannot document all trades can pick and choose what trades to document.

Answer: 2

Losses force traders to stretch their minds and learn new things. It is important to study all aspects of a trade and document your entry while the details are still fresh in your mind. An active trader who can record only some trades needs a disciplined system, such as recording every second, fifth, or even tenth trade, regardless of whether that trade was a winner or a loser.

Question 22—Diary Entry

The diary of an entry into a trade must include all of the following, except:

1. The reason for making this trade
2. The buy grade for long or sell grade for short trades
3. Charts of your trading vehicle at the time of the entry
4. The trade grade

Answer: 4

You want to record your reason for entering a trade to help you discover which signals produce better results. It pays to analyze any market in more than one timeframe: one longer-term, another shorter-term, for a deeper understanding of what is happening. If you follow this rule, you will need to save entry charts in more than one timeframe. While you must rate your entry at the end of the day, you won't know your overall trade grade until you close it out.

Question 23—Trading Plan vs. Diary

Which of the following describes the difference between a Trader's Diary and a Trading Plan?

1. Contains charts in two timeframes.
2. The charts are marked up to identify buy or sell signals.
3. The document is named after the stock ticker.
4. Buy or sell grades are recorded.

   Answer: 4

A trading plan uses the same format as the diary. It shows charts in multiple timeframes, marked up with trade signals. They are named in the same way, even though their labels are different. The one difference is that a trading plan cannot include buy or sell grades—you will know them only after you put on a trade.

Question 24—The Monitoring Screen

The window for monitoring stocks in your trading software should include all of the following, except:

1. Key market indexes
2. Your open positions
3. The stocks you consider trading
4. The stocks you have exited

   Answer: 4

It is essential to monitor your open positions, whether long or short. It is also important to keep an eye on key market indexes, such as the Dow or the Nasdaq. Needless to say, you want to keep a short list of stocks you are thinking of trading on the front burner. The stocks you have exited would only clutter your screen. If you do not plan to re-enter them any time soon, move them to a separate window or tab.

Question 25—Comments on the Screen

Keeping your comments about your open positions on the screen is useful for all of the following reasons, except:

1. It reminds you how long you have been in a trade.
2. It helps you see whether you are winning or losing in an open position.
3. It helps you keep track of your profit target and stop-loss order.
4. It helps you measure your performance.

   Answer: 4

If your trading software allows you to write on the screen, take advantage of this feature. Marking your entry date and price will help you see at a glance where you stand in that trade. Marking up your target and stop levels will allow you to be more alert both to trouble and to profit-taking opportunities. What an on-screen note cannot do is measure your performance. That is something to be accomplished in your Trader's Spreadsheet and transferred into your Diary.

Question 26—Pinning a Chart to a Wall

"Margret's method"—pinning a chart to a wall and marking the trading signal for which you will be waiting—has all of the following advantages, except:

1. It forces you to clearly express what price or indicator action you expect.
2. It keeps you from forgetting a plan.
3. Removing the charts from the wall if your plans change helps keep your mind fresh.
4. Keeping charts on a wall ensures that you will act when the time is right.

   Answer: 4

Printing out a chart and marking up the signals that will prompt you to act is an effective way of monitoring your trading ideas. Seeing those charts whenever you approach your desk provides a powerful reminder of your plans. The bulletin board needs to be periodically purged, to prevent it from turning into an archive of old ideas. Still, no system, no matter how logical, will force you to act—only you can supply the motivation.

Question 27—A Trial-Sized Order

Which of the following statements about a "Chihuahua trade"—a trial-sized order designed to draw your attention to a trading opportunity—is correct?

1. There is little difference between an electronic alert and an order for a handful of shares.
2. Chihuahua orders are good for placing stops.
3. Getting a fill on a Chihuahua order forces you to make a decision.
4. Once you have a fill on a trial-sized order, you must bring that trade up to full size.

Answer: 3

There is a huge emotional difference between receiving a fill for a real trade and getting an e-mail reminding you that a certain level has been reached. You are likely to pay attention to the first while dismissing the second as just another claim on your time in the midst of a busy day. Chihuahua orders are good for entering trades but not for stops—when a stop level is reached, it is time to run. Not every Chihuahua trade must be brought up to full size—in some trades you may choose to sell the pup instead.

Question 28—Grading Buys and Sells

Find the incorrect statement about grading buys or sells:

1. The closer you buy to the low of the bar, the better your grade.
2. The closer you sell to the low of the bar, the better your grade.
3. Selling above the midpoint of the bar earns a positive grade.
4. Buying in the lowest quarter of the bar earns an excellent grade.

Answer: 2

You want to buy as near the low of the bar and sell as near the high of the bar as possible. Buying in the top quarter or selling in the bottom quarter of the daily bar is a loser's game; buying below or selling above midpoint is very good, while buying in the bottom quarter or selling in the upper quarter of the daily bar gives you an excellent grade.

Question 29—Grading Completed Trades

Find the correct statement about grading completed trades:

1. Money is a good measure of the quality of each trade.
2. A long-term trend trader can use channels to measure the quality of trades.
3. A trade capturing over 30% of a channel earns an "A."
4. A trade capturing less than 20% of a channel earns a "D."

Answer: 3

Money, reflected in the equity curve of your account, provides a good measure of your overall trading skill, but it is a poor measure of any individual trade. Channels provide a good yardstick for swing trades but a long-term trader needs a different measure, such as the percentage by which he multiplied his capital. The quality of short-term swing trades is best measured by comparing gains to the height of the channel on the daily chart. Capturing at least 30% of that channel earns you an A, 20% a B, 10% a C, while a loss gets a D.

Question 30—Buying

Find the incorrect statement about buying:

1. The principle of value buying is "buy low, sell high."
2. The principle of momentum buying is "buy high, sell even higher."
3. The upper channel line identifies the level of depression and the lower channel line the level of mania in the markets.
4. Momentum trading works well in runaway trends.

Answer: 3

In quiet markets it makes sense to try to buy at or below value and use channels to sell above value. Momentum trading, such as buying upside breakouts, works better in runaway trends. When prices rise above the upper channel line, they identify a flash of unsustainable optimism, a zone of market mania. When they fall below the lower channel line, they identify the zone of fear and pessimism.

Question 31—Value

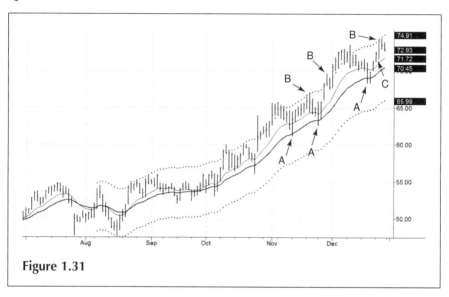

Figure 1.31

Please match the following descriptions with the letters on the chart:

1. Value zone
2. Below value—consider buying
3. Overvalued—consider selling

    Answers: 1. C
                 2. A
                 3. B

If each price is a snapshot, then a moving average is a composite photograph, a reflection of value in the market. If you buy near the moving average, you'll be buying value. If you buy below the EMA, you'll buy undervalued assets. One of the very few scientifically proven facts about the markets is that prices oscillate above and below value. When you sell above the upper channel line, you sell overvalued assets.

Question 32—The Impulse System

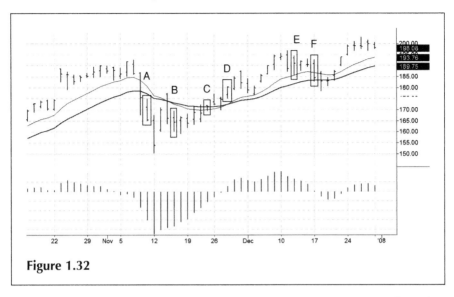

Figure 1.32

The Impulse system tracks both the inertia and the power of market moves. Some software packages allow traders to color price bars in accordance with the Impulse reading. Even on a black-and-white chart, a trader can tell what color any of the bars should be in accordance with the Impulse rules. Please match the following comments on the Impulse system with the letter bars on the chart:

1. Impulse Green—buy or stand aside; shorting not permitted
2. Impulse Red—sell short or stand aside; buying not permitted
3. Impulse Blue—no position is prohibited

Answers: 1. C and D
              2. A and F
              3. B and E

The primary purpose of the Impulse system is that of censorship. It keeps traders out of trouble by telling them what they are prohibited from doing at any given time.

Question 33—The Signals of NH-NL

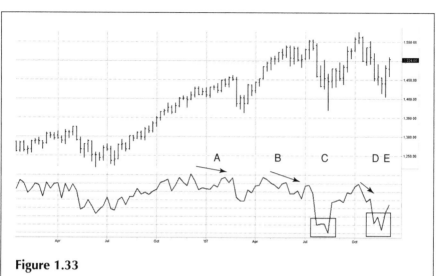

Figure 1.33

The weekly chart of New High–New Low Index (NH-NL) can help traders anticipate important turns in the stock market. Please match the following comments on NH-NL with the letters on the chart:

1. A spike identifies an unsustainable extreme and calls for a reversal.
2. A divergence identifies the weakness of the dominant crowd and calls for a reversal.

Answers: 1. C and E
                2. A, B, and D

Divergences are more often seen at market tops, as the trend keeps rising out of inertia while its leadership becomes weaker. Spikes are much more common at stock market bottoms where they identify zones of panic liquidation. Whenever NH-NL declines to several thousand below zero, a bottom is close at hand.

Question 34—A Trade Diary

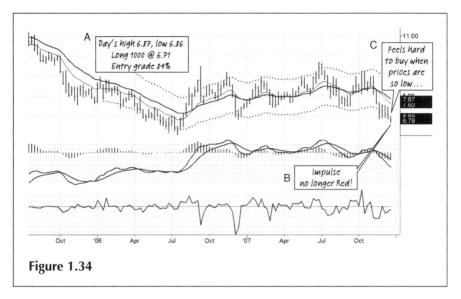

Figure 1.34

This chart comes from a Trader's Diary and illustrates an entry into a trade. Match the following with the letters on the chart:

1. A technical comment on a chart pattern that led to a trade
2. A performance rating
3. A psychological comment

    Answers: 1. **B**
                    2. **A**
                    3. **C**

A visual diary of a trade must include several components. It is essential to mark technical trade signals or comment on the strategy that led to this trade. A Diary must include a quality rating for every entry, exit, and the entire trade. Beginners need to record their feelings during each trade, but more experienced traders tend to become un-emotional about their trades and may skip such comments.

Question 35—Grading a Trade

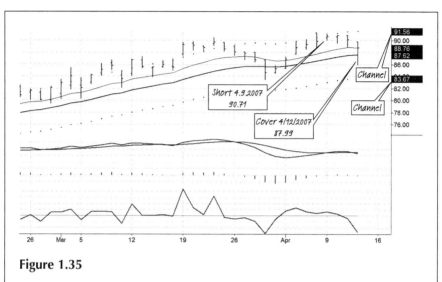

Figure 1.35

This chart shows one of the trades in which I was piggybacking a Spike pick. The weekly chart is not shown here, but you can see bearish divergences of MACD Lines and Force Index on the dailies. The question, however, is about grading this trade: in at 90.71, cover at 87.99, upper channel line at 91.56, lower channel line at 83.67. What is the trade grade?

1. Trade Grade A: Over 30% of the channel
2. Trade Grade B: 20–30% of the channel
3. Trade Grade C: 10–20% of the channel
4. Trade Grade D: Below 10% of the channel

Answer: 1

Shorting at $90.71 and covering at $87.99 gained $2.72, before commissions. The channel was $7.89 tall at the time of the trade. The trade covered 34% of the channel, earning an A grade. It pays to concentrate on points and percentages, and not count money while in a trade.

Question 36—Value Buying vs. Momentum Buying

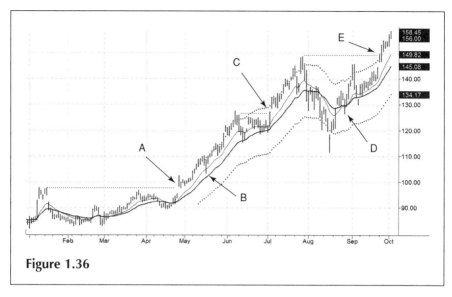

Figure 1.36

Take a look at the letters on this chart and identify which represent value buying or momentum buying zones.

1. Value buying zones
2. Momentum buying zones

> **Answers:**   1. B and D
>   2. A, C, and E

The principle of value buying is "buy low, sell high." The principle of momentum buying is "buy high, sell even higher." Value buying means going long when prices pull back to or below value. Buying on a breakout above an important earlier peak is a prime example of momentum buying. Notice several additional buying opportunities besides those marked with letters on this chart.

GRADING YOUR ANSWERS

If a question requires only one answer, you earn a point by answering it correctly. If a question requires several answers (for example, "Which two of the following four statements are correct?"), rate your answer proportionately. If you answer both correctly, give yourself a point, but if only one, then half a point.

31-36: **Excellent**. You have a good grasp of buying, managing money, and keeping records. Now is the time to turn your attention to selling.

24-30: **Fairly good**. Successful trading demands top performance. Look up the answers to the questions you've missed, review them, and retake the test in a few days before moving on to the next section.

Below 24: **Alarm!** Scoring below the top third may be acceptable in some professional fields, but it is deadly in trading. Professional traders are waiting for you in the markets, ready to take your money. Before you do battle with them, you must bring yourself up to speed. Please study the first section of *Sell and Sell Short* and then retake the test. If your grade remains low on the second pass, look up the books recommended in that section and study those as well.

HOW TO SELL

Question 37—A Plan for Selling

Find the incorrect statement about a written plan for selling:

1. It guarantees success.
2. It reduces stress.
3. It allows you to separate analysis from trading.
4. It makes you less prone to react to the market's zigzags.

Answer: 1

Putting a plan on paper has a powerful psychological effect on most people, making them feel less dependent on the whims of the market. Writing down a plan and executing it from a sheet of paper helps you reduce tension by separating the jobs of analysis and trading. Still, nothing guarantees success in the financial markets.

Question 38—The Three Types of Selling

The three logical types of selling do not include which of the following?

1. Selling at a profit target above the market
2. Selling on a stop below the market
3. Selling in response to the "engine noise" of changing market conditions
4. Selling after feeling impatient about the trade

Answer: 4

Every trading plan should include a profit target and a stop. Furthermore, an experienced discretionary trader may exit a trade in response to "engine noise"—a perception that the market conditions have changed. On the other hand, selling in response to feeling impatient is amateurish.

Question 39—Planning to Sell

Prior to buying a stock, serious traders ask themselves all of the following questions except:

1. How high is the stock likely to rise—what is the profit target?
2. How low does the stock have to fall to activate a protective stop?
3. What is the stock's reward-to-risk ratio?
4. Should I move my target farther away after the stock reaches it?

Answer: 4

Buying a stock is akin to applying for a job—you want to know your responsibilities and rewards, and decide whether the pay is worth the work. The time to think about moving a target will come later in a trade, and even then only for experienced traders.

Question 40—Targets for Selling

Which of the following tools can help set targets for selling?

    A. Moving averages

    B. Envelopes or channels

    C. Support and resistance zones

    D. Other methods

1. A
2. A and B
3. A, B, and C
4. All of the above

Answer: 4

You can use a great variety of methods for setting profit targets. While the range of choices is virtually limitless, two factors are most important. First, you must understand the logic of your target-setting process, and avoid impulsive behavior. Second, you must keep records to help evaluate the quality of any method.

Question 41—A Stock below Its Moving Average

Find two correct statements about a stock that trades below its moving average:

    A. The stock is trading below value.

    B. It is definitely headed lower.

    C. It is definitely headed higher.

    D. If the indicators are pointing higher, the first target is the moving average.

1. A and D
2. B and D
3. A and C
4. A and B

    Answer: 4

A moving average represents an average consensus of value. It indicates the level of value in the current market and its slope shows whether that value is increasing or declining. Nothing is definite in the stock market (except for commissions, slippage, and the fact that an unprepared trader will suffer losses). When the indicators are bullish and price is below the EMA, that EMA becomes the first target for a rally.

Question 42—Moving Averages as Selling Targets

Find the incorrect statement about using moving averages as selling targets:

1. Selling at a moving average works especially well on weekly charts.
2. Prices tend to oscillate above and below their moving averages.
3. It is highly desirable that the distance to the target be longer than the distance to the stop.
4. When you sell at a target, the sell grade is unimportant.

Answer: 4

Time and again, the weekly charts trump the dailies. As a rule, you want to put on trades with attractive reward-to-risk ratios. The quality of entry and exit must be graded for every trade, whatever the reason for the exit.

Question 43—Regrets About Selling

A trader feels intense regret after he sells at an EMA but prices continue to rise. Which of the following statements is correct?

1. Regret is good because it motivates you not to exit the next trade too soon.
2. A strong feeling of regret about exiting early can lead to overstaying the next trade.
3. If your analysis is good, you should know not to sell early.
4. Leaving money on the table is a sign of a poor trader.

Answer: 2

Regret is a corrosive force in trading. If you kick yourself today for leaving some money on the table, you will reach out too far tomorrow and probably overstay your next trade. A mature trader creates a plan and follows it. He grades his performance and strives to improve it. He does not allow the outcome of a trade he made today to impact his behavior in a new trade tomorrow. Leaving some money on the table is an inevitable part of the game; only a paper-trader or a liar catches every bottom and sells at every top.

Question 44—The Timing of a Sale Near the EMA

What is the best time to use an EMA as a target for a rally?

1. When prices rally from bear market lows
2. In the midst of an ongoing uptrend
3. When prices are boiling near their historic highs
4. All of the above

Answer: 1

The time to use an EMA as a price target is when prices are below that EMA. This is unlikely to happen in an uptrend or near the highs. When prices rally from bear market lows, an EMA serves as a reasonable target for the first rally.

Question 45—Channels as Price Targets

Find the correct statement about using channels as price targets:

1. A powerful upmove on the weekly charts is the best time to target channels on the dailies.
2. Uptrends rarely show an orderly pattern of tops and bottoms.
3. The best time to go long in an uptrend is when prices hit the upper channel.
4. It does not pay to sell at a channel because prices may rally higher.

Answer: 1

An orderly pattern of rallies and declines is fairly typical during major uptrends. This is why it makes sense to trade by going long whenever prices drop to or below value and take profits whenever they rise to or above an overvalued zone, as identified by the upper channel line. It pays to sell when and where you plan to sell. You may plan to sell a short-term trade at the channel line or hold a smaller position for a longer, trend-following trade. Whatever your plan, do not change it in the middle of the game!

Question 46—Measuring Performance Using Channels

Measuring the percentage of a channel height captured in a trade can help a swing trader:

A. Focus on points rather than dollars.
B. Provide a yardstick for measuring one's progress.
C. Set a realistic profit target.

1. A
2. A and B
3. All of the above

Answer: 3

Focusing on money gained or lost in any given trade tends to distract traders. It is important to focus on the quality of trading decisions; paying too much attention to money leads one towards thinking about what that money will buy, and then the trader loses his focus. The goal is to become the best trader you can be—the money will follow.

Question 47—Selling Targets

Please find statements that match among the following two pairs of statements:

    A. The first target for selling into a rally off the lows

    B. The first target for selling in an ongoing uptrend

1. At or below value, as defined by moving averages
2. Near the overvalued zone, as defined by the upper channel line

    Answers: 1. A
                   2. B

The first rally from bear market lows tends to run into great resistance; it makes sense to set a modest profit target near the EMA. Prices seldom fall to the lower channel line in an ongoing uptrend; it makes sense to buy near the EMA and be prepared to take profits near the upper channel line.

Question 48—Reaching for a Greater Profit

Always reaching out for a greater profit makes a trader:

    A. More relaxed

    B. More stressed

    C. More successful

    D. More hyperactive

1. A and B
2. A and C
3. B and D
4. B and C

Answer: 3

One of the great psychological problems in trading is that the markets offer endless temptations. With thousands of dollars flashing on every screen, many traders lose self-control and reach for more than they can catch, before losing balance and suffering losses. The power word in trading, as in life, is "enough." Using a trading channel to set profit targets can help establish realistic goals for trades.

Question 49—The Top of a Rally

Find the correct statement about the top tick of a rally:

1. Forecasting it will provide a reasonable target for selling.
2. It can be forecast with a good degree of consistency.
3. Trying to sell at the top tick tends to be a very expensive undertaking.
4. If one can sell consistently at the absolute top, one can also sell short there.

Answer: 3

The top tick of a rally is the most expensive tick in the market—fortunes have been lost hunting for it. Here, as with everything else in trading, it is important to avoid reaching for extremes. It is much safer and more practical to try and take a chunk out of the middle of a price move. The less you stress yourself, the better results you're likely to get.

Question 50—Prices above the Upper Channel Line

Assume that prices have rallied above the upper channel line; find the correct statement among the following:

1. A trader must immediately take profits.
2. When prices close above the upper channel line for two days in a row, a trader must take profits.
3. When prices close above the upper channel line, it means the rally will continue.
4. When prices close above the upper channel line but then fail to reach a new high, the trader should consider selling that day.

Answer: 4

Envelopes or channels provide good targets for short-term trades. Still, occasionally a rally rockets higher, tempting us to hold on for a bit longer than initially planned. A very powerful rally may cause a stock to "walk its channel line," rising along that line for days and sometimes weeks. Still, a short-term swing trader would be well advised to sell when that rally stumbles and fails to reach a new high after having risen above the upper channel line.

Question 51—Setting Profit Targets

Find the correct statement about setting profit targets:

1. Let the trade run as far as it will without worrying about targets.
2. There is a perfect profit target for any market.
3. The longer your time horizon, the farther away the profit target.
4. A moving average provides the best profit target for any trade.

Answer: 3

A market can move much farther in the long run than in the short run—a short-term swing trade needs a close-by target, while a long-term trend trade needs a target farther away. There is no universal method that will set a price target for every trade.

Question 52—Support and Resistance Zones as Targets

Support and resistance zones provide attractive price targets for long-term trades for all of the following reasons, except:

1. Congestion zones show where the masses of market participants are prepared to buy or sell.
2. A trading range represents a general consensus of value among huge masses of traders.
3. The duration of trading ranges tends to be longer than that of price trends.
4. A trend always stops at the edge of a trading range.

Answer: 4

A price range represents a huge financial and emotional commit-ment by masses of buyers and sellers. The composition and the atti-tude of the market crowd keep shifting, which is why the edges of congestion zones tend to be ragged rather than straight.

Question 53—A Protective Stop

Using a protective stop makes sense for all of the following reasons, except:

1. It is a reality check, reminding you that prices can move against you.
2. It works against the ownership effect, when people fall in love with their stocks.
3. It reduces the emotional stress of making decisions in open trades.
4. It puts an absolute limit on the amount of dollars you can lose in any given trade.

Answer: 4

Prior to entering a trade you need to examine the chart and decide where you want to get out if that trade starts going against you. Your decision is likely to be much more objective if you make it before entering a trade. Every trade deserves a protective stop—but a stock may gap across that level. A stop is not a perfect defense but it is our best defense against damaging losses.

Question 54—Breaking through Resistance

If a stock rises to its resistance level, stays there, and then rallies and closes above that level, it gives us a signal to:

    A. Go long immediately.
    B. Get ready to sell short if the stock sinks back into its resistance zone.
    C. Sell short immediately.
    D. Get ready to buy if the stock declines towards its resistance zone.

1. A or D
2. A or B
3. B or C
4. C or D

Answer: 2

Prices breaking out above resistance may either signal the beginning of a new uptrend or the first step in a fakeout move. If the breakout is for real, there is no time to waste. It does not pay to wait for a pull-back—a rocket that has left its launching pad has no business sinking back to it. If, on the other hand, your long-term studies point to a top and you think this is a false breakout, it makes sense to wait for a con-firmation from prices sinking back into the range. A breakout alone does not provide a clear signal—it pays to view it within the frame-work of your longer-term studies.

Question 55—A Trade without a Stop
A trade without a stop is:

1. Permitted only for experienced traders
2. A gamble
3. A way to be more flexible
4. A realistic approach to trading

Answer: 2

A stop is every trader's link with reality. There are many types of stops and many methods of using them, but even the most experi-enced professional trader knows at what level he will exit a trade that is going against him.

Question 56—Changing Stops
Which of the following are allowed during a trade?

   A. Raising stops on longs
   B. Raising stops on shorts
   C. Lowering stops on shorts
   D. Lowering stops on longs

1. A and B
2. B and C
3. A and C
4. C and D

Answer: 3

You may move a stop only in the direction of a trade—up for longs or down for shorts. Moving a stop in the opposite direction in order to give a trade gone bad "more room to work out" is a loser's game. You created your plan before you entered the trade, when you were more objective than during the trade. Once you are in a trade, you are allowed to reduce your risk level but never to increase it.

Question 57—Re-Entering a Trade

Buying a stock, getting stopped out, and then re-entering the trade by buying that stock back is:

1. A common tactic among professionals
2. Throwing good money after bad
3. A sign of stubbornness
4. A waste of time and money that could be spent on better opportunities

Answer: 1

Beginners usually take a single stab at a stock and move on to the next trade after a loss. A professional knows that a good stock is hard to find. He or she uses a tight stop and is not afraid to make several stabs at a stock before catching an important trend.

Question 58—Deciding Where to Set a Stop

The single most important question in setting a stop is:

1. What is the volatility of the market you are trading?
2. How much money are you prepared to risk?
3. What is your profit target?
4. How many shares are you planning to buy?

Answer: 2

Setting stops is an integral part of risk control and money management. Prior to entering a trade you must decide how much money you are trying to make and how much you are prepared to risk in reaching your goal. Gauging possible profits and current volatility is very important but all questions ultimately boil down to defining what risk you'll be ready to accept.

Question 59—The Impact of the Last Trade

What impact should the size of your latest profit or loss have on your plans for the next trade?

1. Trade a bigger size after a profitable trade.
2. Trade a smaller size after an unprofitable trade.
3. Trade a bigger size after an unprofitable trade.
4. None of the above

   Answer: 4

Allowing the results of your latest trade to influence your plans for the next is amateurish behavior. There is a fair degree of randomness in the market, making the outcome of any single trade difficult to predict. A professional puts his trust not in any individual trade but in his or her ongoing performance over a period of time. The pros do not let something as relatively minor as the outcome of the latest trade make them deviate from their thought-out plans.

Question 60—"The Iron Triangle"

Please match the components of "The Iron Triangle" of risk control with their descriptions:

   A. Money management
   B. Stop placement
   C. Position sizing

1. Set it on the basis of chart analysis.
2. Decide how much money you will risk in this trade.
3. Divide one of the three factors by another.

Answer: 1. B
2. A
3. C

Stops are set on the basis of chart analysis. Your money management rules will give you the maximum amount of dollars you may risk in this trade, although you may want to risk less. Dividing this number by the dollar risk per share gives you the size of the trade.

Question 61—A Limit Order

A limit order is preferable to a market order for all of the following reasons except:

1. It prevents slippage.
2. It guarantees execution.
3. It works best for entering trades.
4. It is useful for taking profits at target levels.

Answer: 2

Only a market order guarantees an execution. A limit order, on the other hand, demands a fill at a specific price or better—or no execution at all. It helps you avoid slippage, one of the major but seldom recognized causes of poor performance among traders. The only time not to quibble about slippage is when you are trying to get out of a trade that is going against you. That's why it pays to use market orders for stops.

Question 62—Soft Stops

Which of the following statements about soft stops is correct?

1. They are very useful for system traders.
2. They offer a good way to get started in the markets.
3. They help avoid whipsaws.
4. They are easier to set than hard stops.

Answer: 3

A hard stop goes into the market as a specific order. A soft stop is the number you keep in your head. System traders must use hard stops, as do all beginning traders. Experienced discretionary traders may use soft stops in order to reduce whipsaws. Both hard and soft stops take the same amount of work and belong on the same level— their placement is identical, only the execution is different.

Question 63—A Stop One Tick below the Latest Low

Putting a protective stop on a long position one tick below the latest low is problematic for all of the following reasons, except:

1. Even a small sell order thrown at the market near the lows can briefly push it below the latest low.
2. A bullish pattern occurs when a market takes out its previous low by a small margin and reverses.
3. Professionals like to fade (trade against) breakouts.
4. Once the low is taken out, prices are likely to decline much lower.

Answer: 4

The trouble with putting a stop a penny below the latest low is that markets very often trace out double bottoms, with the second bottom slightly lower than the first. The level immediately below the latest low is where amateurs cut and run and where professionals tend to buy. Once in a while prices take out the previous low and go into a waterfall decline—but that is an exception rather than a rule. It is essential to use stops, but there are much better ways to place them than one tick below the latest low.

Question 64—A Stop at the Level of the Previous Low

Placing a stop exactly at the level of the previous low can be good for all of the following reasons, except:

1. A downtrend often slows down as it approaches the level of the previous low.
2. If the stock declines to its previous low, it is likely to go even lower.
3. Stocks often accelerate immediately after taking the previous low.
4. Slippage tends to be higher when the stop is at the level of the previous low rather than one tick below that low.

Answer: 4

If you put a stop at the exact level of the previous low and that stop gets hit, your slippage is likely to be lower than in the case of a stop a tick below that low. Stocks often accelerate after taking out their previous low, causing greater slippage on stops below. Your risk of a whipsaw increases only very slightly—if the stock falls to that level, it is virtually certain to go a tick lower.

Question 65—A Stop That Is "Tighter by a Day"

Find the correct statement about a stop that is "tighter by a day" ("Nic's Stop"):

1. Examine the bars that bracket a recent low and place your stop a little below the lower of those two bars.
2. Using a tight stop is not suitable for short-term trading.
3. This method is especially useful for long-term position trades.
4. A tight stop like this one eliminates slippage.

Answer: 1

Placing a stop inside the recent trading range is designed for short-term swing trading. It tells the market to "put up or shut up." Still, no stop order can ever completely eliminate slippage.

Question 66—Trade Duration

The outcome of a trade depends in part on the duration of that trade. Find the incorrect statement about the impact of trade duration:

1. Longer-term trades give you the luxury of time to think and make decisions.
2. If a day-trader stops to think, he loses.
3. The more time a stock has, the farther it can move.
4. Long-term position trades provide the best learning experience.

Answer: 4

Time is a hugely important factor in trading. The more time a market has, the farther it can move, increasing both the profit opportunities and the risk of an adverse move. A trader with a longer-term orientation can stop to think, unlike a day-trader who must react almost automatically. The best way to learn to trade is by making many small trades; the slower pace of long-term trading does not provide as good a learning experience as shorter-term swing trading.

Question 67—Wider Stops

Find the correct statement about using wider stops:

1. A major uptrend is less volatile than a minor one.
2. The wider the stop, the greater the risk of a whipsaw.
3. A stop belongs outside of the zone of the normal chop of prices.
4. The wider the stop, the larger position you can carry.

Answer: 3

Prices meander, and the more time they have, the wider their swing. The tighter the stop, the greater the risk of a whipsaw. The whole point of using wider stops is to put them outside the zone of the normal chop of prices. The downside of using a wider stop is that by accepting greater risk per share you reduce the size of the position you can carry.

Question 68—Moving Stops

Which of the following statements about moving stops is incorrect?

1. You may move stops only in the direction of the trade but never against it.
2. When you switch to a trailing stop after the prices reach their target you increase your risk.
3. When prices hang just above your stop, it makes sense to lower it to reduce the risk of a whipsaw.
4. When prices move in your favor, it makes sense to raise your stop to protect a part of your paper profit.

Answer: 3

No matter how strong the temptation to make your stop wider, you must stick with your original decision. If prices move your way, you may well adjust your stop to protect a part of your paper profit. If prices reach your target but you want to stay in the trade, you may switch to a trailing stop; reaching for a greater profit means accepting the risk of giving back some of the existing profit if the trend reverses on you.

Question 69—The SafeZone Stops

Find the correct statement about the SafeZone stop:

1. It acts as a filter that suppresses the signal of the trend.
2. Noise is any part of today's range that protrudes outside of the previous day's range.
3. SafeZone tracks Average Upside Penetration in uptrends and Average Downside Penetration in downtrends.
4. SafeZone works best during trends and worst during trading ranges.

Answer: 4

The purpose of SafeZone is to suppress noise so that the signal of the trend can come through. The noise is that part of the day's range which protrudes outside of yesterday's range but only in the direction opposite to the trend. For example, when the trend is up, upside penetrations are normal, while downside penetrations are considered noise. When the trend is down, downside penetrations are normal while upside penetrations are considered noise. SafeZone tracks Average Downside Penetrations during uptrends and Average Upside Penetrations in downtrends and sets up stops outside of the noise level. Like many other methods, it works best during trends but leads to whipsaws during trading ranges.

Question 70—Trading with the SafeZone

Which of the following statements about SafeZone stops is incorrect?

1. SafeZone is a mechanical trading system.
2. You have to establish the lookback period for the SafeZone.
3. You need to choose the coefficient by which to multiply the normal noise to obtain the SafeZone stop.
4. Usually, a coefficient between two and three provides a margin of safety.

Answer: 1

To use SafeZone one must establish its lookback period and the co-efficient by which to multiply the normal noise to obtain the SafeZone stop. Setting that coefficient must be done individually for every market—hardly a mechanical approach to trading.

Question 71—The Volatility-Drop Method

Which of the following statements about the Volatility-Drop method is incorrect?

1. A Volatility-Drop ensures getting greater profit from every trade.
2. This methods allows a trader to start out with a modest target, but reach out for more while in the trade.
3. Using a Volatility-Drop stop involves risking some of the paper profit.
4. Using this method helps automate profit-taking decisions.

Answer: 1

Kerry Lovvorn, the author of this method, says "I do not think of using a trailing stop until my target is hit. At that time the trade has fulfilled its duty, but the market may be moving in a way that seems to have potential for an additional reward." The Volatility-Drop method puts some of the existing profit at risk to squeeze more money out of the trade but it does not guarantee that every trade will become more profitable as a result.

Question 72—"Engine Noise" in the Markets

Selling "engine noise" refers to selling when:

1. Your target is reached.
2. Your stop is hit.
3. You want to take partial profits.
4. You do not like how the market is acting.

Answer: 4

A discretionary trader does not have to hold every trade to its planned target. Perhaps the market wants to give you less than you initially expected. If you see signals of the trend weakening, it could be a wise decision to sell sooner than originally planned.

Question 73—Selling "Engine Noise"

Which statement about selling "engine noise" is incorrect?

1. A system trader may not sell "engine noise."
2. A discretionary trader may exit the market sooner or later than planned.
3. Selling "engine noise" is especially well suited for beginning traders.
4. Selling "engine noise" carries a risk of cutting profits.

Answer: 3

While selling at profit targets or using protective stops works for traders at all levels of expertise, selling in response to "engine noise" requires a much greater level of experience. There is a very real risk that a trader, especially an inexperienced one, will sell too soon out of boredom or anxiety.

Question 74—Not Liking Market's Action

You are holding a long position but do not like the toppy signals of indicators. Which statement about the courses of action open to you is incorrect?

1. If you are a system trader, you must hold your position as planned.
2. If you are a discretionary trader, you may sell your position.
3. If you are a system trader, you may switch to a different system that allows an earlier exit.
4. If you are a discretionary trader, you may take partial profits but retain the core position.

Answer: 3

A system must be followed. Using your discretion to change to a different system in the middle of a trade means that you are no longer a system trader. Exiting a trade or reducing its size in response to "engine noise" is the privilege and the responsibility of a discretionary trader. A system trader may anticipate some of the "noises" and incorporate them into his system—but not change that system while in an open trade.

Question 75—Earnings Reports

Which statement about the impact of earnings reports is incorrect?

1. Prices are largely driven by the anticipation of future earnings.
2. An earnings report never changes a long-term stock trend.
3. Earnings reports rarely come as a surprise to professional watchers.
4. Insider trading is usually linked to the way a company is managed.

   Answer: 2

When we buy a stock we are paying for future earnings and dividends. Insiders have the best knowledge of those factors and many of them profit from it. Stocks seldom jump on earnings reports because smart bulls have already bought or clever bears have already sold. Still, the stock of an honestly run company can change its trend following a surprising earnings report.

Question 76—The Market "Rings a Bell"

The market "rings a bell" when:

1. It makes a multiyear high.
2. It falls to a multiyear low.
3. An event occurs far outside the norm for this market.
4. The market flashes a signal anyone can recognize.

Answer: 3

You hear the market bell when you recognize an event so far outside the norm that it may seem as if the laws of the market have been cancelled. In fact the laws of the market cannot go away, any more than the law of gravity can. An extraordinary event is a sign of a bubble ready to burst. This behavior is very clear only in retrospect, but during the bubble it seems perfectly normal; only a cool and objective trader can hear this bell.

Question 77—Trading with the New High–New Low Index

Which statement about the New High–New Low Index (NH-NL) is incorrect?

1. When NH-NL is above zero it shows that bulls are stronger than bears.
2. New Highs are the leaders in weakness and New Lows are the leaders in strength.
3. Bearish divergences are commonly seen near the ends of bull markets.
4. A severe downspike of weekly NH-NL usually signals a market bottom.

Answer: 2

New Highs are the leaders in strength—they are the stocks that have reached their highest point for the past 52 weeks on any given day. New Lows are the leaders in weakness—the stocks that have reached their lowest point for the past 52 weeks on that day. Tops and bottoms in the stock market tend to be asymmetrical. Tops are formed more slowly and often show bearish divergences of NH-NL. Bottoms are formed faster and often marked by panicky downspikes of NH-NL as losers dump their shares on the market, creating an opportunity for savvy bulls.

Question 78—A Decision-Making Tree vs. a Trading System

The key difference between a decision-making tree and a trading system is that only one of them includes:

1. The rules for entering a trade
2. The rules for exiting a trade
3. The permission to bend your exit rules
4. The parameters for trade sizing

Answer: 3

A good trading system is totally objective—if you give it to two different traders, both should come up with the same entries, exits, and trade sizes. The decision-making tree of a discretionary trader also addresses entries, exits, and trade sizing, but it permits some flexibility in applying those rules.

Question 79—A Decision-Making Tree

Which of the following questions does not belong in a decision-making tree:

1. Is this a short-term or a long-term trade?
2. Where will you place your stop?
3. What kind of "engine noise" will you listen to while in a trade?
4. What kind of record-keeping will you perform for a trade?

Answer: 4

Good record-keeping is extremely important—it is the foundation of successful trading. The records of a serious trader must address the issues of record-keeping, choice of software, and psychology. Decision-making trees are built on this foundation but deal with specific trading issues, such as entries, exits, and position sizing.

Question 80—Value Buying and Selling Targets

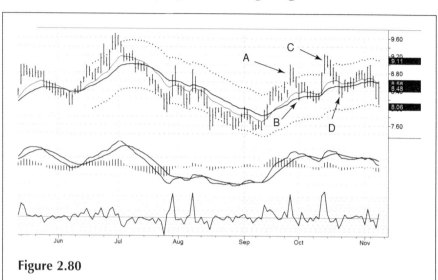

Figure 2.80

Please identify value buying zones and selling targets among the letter points on this chart:

1. Value buying zones
2. Selling targets in overvalued zones

> **Answer:**   1.   B and D
>   2.   A and C

In a steady uptrend, it pays to go long near value, as defined by moving averages, and take profits in the overvalued zone, above the upper channel line. Note that markets have quite a bit of noise, and the best signals are clearly visible only in retrospect. For example, after buying at point D, prices never reached the upper channel line and eventually slid lower. People who seek perfection feel overwhelmed by such turns, while mature traders protect themselves with good money management and charge ahead.

Question 81—Support, Resistance, and Targets

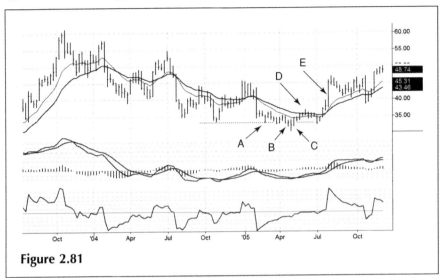

Figure 2.81

Please match the following descriptions with the letters on the chart.

1. Line of support broken
2. Prices close above support, giving a signal to buy
3. Support established
4. Second seling target at the upper channel line
5. First selling target at the EMA

   Answer: 1. B   2. C   3. A   4. E   5. D

A false downside breakout, accompanied by a bullish divergence is one of the strongest signals in technical analysis. Once prices break below an important support line, you need to watch very closely what happens next: Will the decline accelerate or will the break fizzle out? When a price bar closes above the previously broken line of support it gives a powerful buy signal. Here this signal was reinforced by a bullish divergence of MACD-Histogram. Notice the pullback to support between points D and E, which provided an excellent opportunity to hop aboard the long trade. You cannot count on such pullbacks happening very often; they are an exception rather than the rule.

Question 82—Multiple Targets

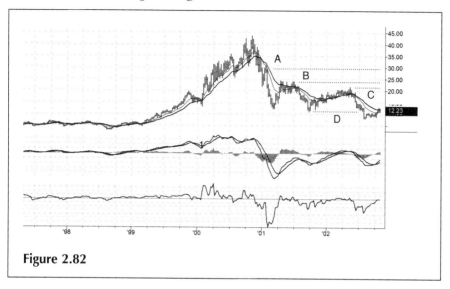

Figure 2.82

Please match the following descriptions with the letters on this monthly chart:

1. The minimal price target
2. Support
3. The bull market target

Answer: 1. B   2. D   3. A

Line D identifies the zone of major support, the floor of a vicious bear market. Near the right edge of the chart prices broke below support but then, instead of falling any lower, reversed and closed above support. A false downside breakout, coupled with a bullish divergence of MACD, provided a major buy signal. Since we are looking at a monthly chart, it is reasonable to expect a major move—the longer the timeframe, the greater the forecast. If we expect a new bull market to begin, then line C, drawn across the top of the most recent rally, is not even a target—it is too close. Line B, drawn across the top of the previous major rally, provides a minimal measurement for the upmove. Line A, drawn across the bottom area of the all-time top, provides a more reasonable target for the bullish move, although reaching that height will require patience. The stock eventually exceeded its previous peak, rising to a new all-time high.

Question 83—Holding, Adding, or Profit-Taking

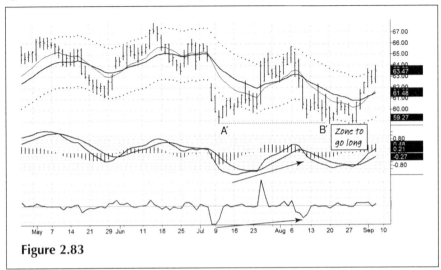

Figure 2.83

At point **A′** the stock declined to 58.78. At point **B′** it fell to 58.71 but recoiled from its new low. This false downside breakout was accompanied by bullish divergences in several indicators. If a trader went long with a target near the upper channel line, which of the following actions are legitimate at the right edge of this chart?

    A. Sell and take profits.
    B. Sell half, hold half.
    C. Continue to hold, tighten the stop.
    D. Add to the winning position.

1. A
2. A or B
3. A, B, or C
4. All of the above

    Answer: 3

    A false downside breakout, coupled with a series of bullish divergences provides a powerful buy signal. A system trader or a beginning discretionary trader must take profits at the target, in this case the upper channel line. A more experienced discretionary trader is allowed to hold out for more, depending on his judgment. It would make no sense for a value trader to add to his position near the upper channel line, in the overvalued zone.

Question 84—Handling a Profitable Trade

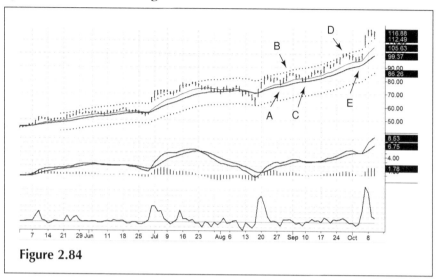

Figure 2.84

A trader recognizes an uptrend and starts buying the stock near value, selling near the upper channel line. He goes long at point **A** and sells at **B**, long at point **C** and sells at **D**, long again at point **E**. When prices gap above the upper channel line he decides to hold for a greater gain. What is the wise course of action at the right edge of this chart?

1. Sell and take profits.
2. Sell half the position.
3. Hold the position.
4. Add to the position.

Answer: 1

When a rally goes vertical, it is extremely difficult to forecast where it will end. At the rightmost bar on the chart we see that, for the first time since the stock blew through its upper channel line, it failed to reach a new high. This reduction of momentum flashes a signal to take your money and go home. Additional support for this decision is provided by MACD-Histogram which has reached a level consistent with tops. Also, you can see here that the tall peaks of Force Index are usually followed by a period of flat prices rather than a continuation of an uptrend.

Question 85—Placing a Stop

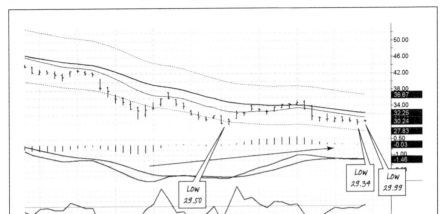

Figure 2.85

A trader recognizes a bullish divergence accompanied by a false down-side breakout. He decides to go long, but needs to place a stop. At which of the following levels would he be advised to place it?

1. 29.49
2. 29.33
3. 29.34
4. 29.98
5. 28.99

Answer: 3

A stop needs to be placed fairly close to prices, but not so close as to get into the zone of normal market noise; 29.34 marks the lowest point of the latest downmove. Putting a stop at this level tells the market to "put up or shut up"—a strong buy signal should lead to a quick rally; if the signal fails, there is no reason to give that stock extra time. Putting the stop a penny lower, at 29.33 would risk slippage—once the bottom tick is taken out, prices tend to go flying, leading to gaps and slippage. Placing the stop below the low of the last trading day in such a flat market would mean getting into the zone of normal market noise.

Question 86—The Decision at the Right Edge of the Chart

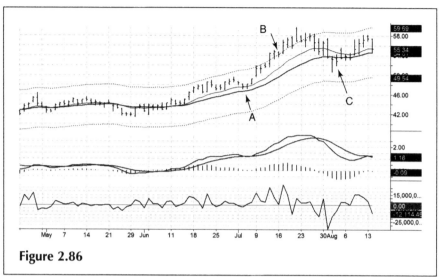

Figure 2.86

A trader recognizes an uptrend and goes long at point **A**. He sells at point **B**, after prices blow out of their channel but then fail to make a new high. He buys again at point **C**, after prices decline below value and stop making new lows. What would be the reasonable course of action at the right edge of this chart?

1. Continue to hold.
2. Add to long position.
3. Sell.

Answer: 3

At the right edge of the chart the trade continues on track, showing a small profit. There are, however, disturbing technical signs. The primary sign of danger for the bulls is a severe bearish divergence of MACD-Histogram. At point A, the indicator rallied in gear with price, confirming the upmove. At point B prices returned to the top area, but the indicator barely rose above the zero line, pointing to a severe weakness of the bulls. This kind of "engine noise" coming from the market provides a signal that the uptrend is weak and it is better to get out of a long trade.

GRADING YOUR ANSWERS

If a question requires only one answer, you earn a point by answering it correctly. If a question requires several answers (for example, "Which two of the following four statements are correct?"), rate your answer proportionately. If you answer both correctly, give yourself a point, but if only one, then half a point.

43–50: Excellent. You have a good grasp of selling. Now is the time to turn your attention to selling short.

35–42: Fairly good. Successful trading demands top performance. Look up the answers to the questions you've missed, review them, and retake the test in a few days before moving on to the next section.

Below 35: Alarm! Not being able to perform in the top third may be acceptable in many professional fields, but not in trading. The competition is just too intense to accept this result. Before you go into the markets, you must bring yourself up to speed. Please study the second section of *Sell and Sell Short* and retake the test. If your grade remains low on the second pass, look up the books recommended in that section and study them before retaking the test.

How to Sell Short

Question 87—Shorting a Stock

Selling a stock short means:

1. Selling an overvalued stock from your portfolio
2. Selling a borrowed stock
3. Selling a stock in a severe downtrend
4. Selling a stock you expect to be delisted

Answer: 2

There are many reasons to sell a stock—you may think that it is overvalued or about to decline. While these reasons can apply to any stock, there is only one way to sell a stock short—by borrowing its shares. People who sell short reverse the standard process of buying first and selling later. Shorts begin by selling borrowed shares in order to buy them back later. This allows them to profit from stock declines rather than rallies.

Question 88—Risk Factors in Shorting

The major risk factors in selling short include all of the following, except:

1. A stock might rally.
2. A stock might issue a dividend.
3. A stock might be called back by the owner.
4. A stock might crash.

Answer: 4

A crash is profitable for shorts, whereas a rally leads to a loss. If the company whose stock a trader sold short declares a dividend, it goes to the person who bought that stock. Now the short-seller must reimburse the owner, whose shares he borrowed, for the cost of that dividend. If the owner decides to sell his stock and the broker cannot find another owner willing to lend his stock to a short-seller, that short-seller will be forced to cover earlier than planned in order to return the borrowed shares.

Question 89—The Impact of Shorting

People who sell stocks short help create a more orderly market through all of the following, except:

1. Dampening price increases
2. Cushioning price declines
3. Increasing price swings
4. Dampening volatility

Answer: 3

Short-sellers sell into rallies, increasing supply when prices are high. They cover during price breaks, thus cushioning them. By trading against the crowd, which is almost uniformly long, short-sellers help dampen excessive price swings.

Question 90—Short vs. Long

The main advantage of shorting over buying is that:

1. Tops are easier to recognize than bottoms.
2. Stocks fall faster than they rise.
3. It is easier to sell into a rally than buy into a decline.
4. Stocks rise faster than they fall.

Answer: 2

The great advantage of selling stocks short is that they tend to go down about twice as fast as they rise. This applies to all timeframes—to monthly, weekly, daily, as well as intraday charts. It takes buying to put the stocks up but they can fall under their own weight. Nothing is really "easy" in the markets, whether selling tops or buying bottoms.

Question 91—Disadvantages of Shorting

The greatest disadvantage in shorting stocks is that the stock market:

1. Keeps fluctuating
2. Has relatively slow rises and fast declines
3. Rises over time
4. Has an uptick rule

Answer: 3

The one great disadvantage of shorting stocks is that the broad stock market has a centuries-old tendency to rise over time. The estimates vary, but an average 3% rise per year above the rate of inflation seems like a reasonable estimate. This means that in shorting you are swimming against a gently rising tide. To deal with this, you want to be more short-term oriented in shorting than in buying. The uptick rule is no longer in effect in the United States.

Question 92—Learning to Sell Short

Which statement about learning to sell short is incorrect?

1. Find a stock you'd hate to own.
2. Trade a large size to make the experience worthwhile.
3. Avoid shorting stocks making new highs.
4. Look for expensive stocks.

Answer: 2

When learning to short, think of the stocks you expect to decline and zero in on those you would hate to own. If it makes sense to buy low and sell high, then more expensive stocks are likely to produce good shorting candidates. When you go long, it is not a good idea to buy a stock that keeps making new lows. Similarly, when you want to go short it is not a good idea to sell a stock that keeps making new highs. Trade size serves as a huge emotional amplifier—the bigger the size, the greater the stress. Make your first baby steps while trading a size so small that neither gain nor loss will matter much at all—this will allow you to focus on quality.

Question 93—Shorting vs. Buying

Find the correct statement among the following comparisons of buying and shorting:

1. Tops take longer to form than bottoms.
2. Stock bottoms are built on hope and greed.
3. Precise timing is more important in buying than shorting.
4. Fear is the dominant emotion of stock tops.

   Answer: 1

Stock market bottoms tend to be narrow and sharp, while the tops tend to be broad and uneven. Stock market bottoms are built on fear, a sharp and powerful emotion. Tops are built on greed, a happy emotion that can last a long time. Since the declines tend to occur faster than rallies, precise timing is more important in shorting.

Question 94—Shorting Stock Market Tops

Which statement about shorting stock market tops is incorrect?

1. Stops need to be placed relatively farther away, due to high volatility.
2. Wider stops require larger positions.
3. There is nothing wrong with trying to re-enter a trade after getting stopped out.
4. Trading positions smaller than the maximum allowed by money management rules increase holding power.

Answer: 2

When prices are boiling near the top, you can expect high volatility and wide price swings. As a result, stops are hard to place. The wider the stops, the greater your risk per share. As the risk per share increases, the size of the position must be reduced. It is not uncommon to take several stabs at shorting a top before catching a big break. Reducing the size of your position below the maximum dictated by money management rules increases your holding power.

Question 95—Shorting in Downtrends

Find the correct statement regarding shorting in downtrends:

1. Shorting in the middle of a channel means shorting above value.
2. Covering near the lower channel line means buying below value.
3. There is only one good shorting opportunity within a channel.
4. Grading your trades by the percentage of a channel does not work for shorting.

Answer: 2

In the middle of a channel prices are near value. The time to cover shorts and take profits is when prices fall to the undervalued zone near the lower channel line. Channels often provide multiple trading opportunities, as prices keep rising to value only to collapse below value again and again. Grading swing trades by the percentage of a channel captured in that trade works equally well for longs and shorts.

Question 96—The Tactics of Shorting Downtrends

Find the incorrect statement about shorting in downtrends:

1. Make a strategic decision on the weekly chart, make tactical plans on the daily.
2. Shorting within a channel lowers both the risk and the potential rewards.
3. Shorting within a channel increases the risk of a whipsaw.
4. A single short within a channel will not catch a major move.

Answer: 3

The risk of a whipsaw is the greatest when trying to short a market top. Shorting within a channel reduces the risk of a whipsaw. Nothing is free in the markets, and one pays for reduced risk by a corresponding reduction in potential profits—those are greater when shorting tops and relatively smaller in downtrends.

Question 97—Shorting the Fundamentals

Find the correct statement about shorting on the basis of fundamental information:

1. A fundamental analyst can cover more markets than a technician.
2. One can use technical studies as an idea generator and fundamentals as a trigger.
3. Fundamental information overrides technical factors.
4. The most powerful situation exists when the fundamentals suggest a trade and technical factors confirm that signal.

Answer: 4

Fundamental analysis is narrower than technical analysis because of the economic differences between various markets; a technician can apply his tools across the board. Fundamental ideas must be verified with technical analysis. No matter how good a fundamental story, if the technical factors do not confirm it, there is no trade. When both point in the same direction, they create a very powerful combination.

Question 98—Looking for Shorting Candidates

Which of the following is not a valid method of looking for shorting candidates?

1. Looking at the weakest stock industry groups
2. Listening to rumors and tips, then checking them using your analytic method
3. Looking for the weakest stocks among the Nasdaq 100
4. Selling short stocks that are being upgraded by major analysts

Answer: 4

There are just as many methods of looking for shorting as for buying candidates. The key principle is to verify any idea using your own method or system. You may do something as labor-intensive as digging through industry groups or the 100 biggest stocks on the Nasdaq; alternatively, you may do something as simple as listening to tips, rumors, or downgrade news. Anything can provide grist for the mill—as long as you test all tips and ideas using your analytic method.

Question 99—The Short Interest Ratio

The Short Interest Ratio reflects the intensity of shorting by measuring:

1. The number of shares held short by the bears relative to the "free float."
2. The number of stocks shorted by a trader relative to the number of shares he bought.
3. The number of traders holding shorts relative to the number of traders holding longs.
4. The number of traders whose accounts are set up for shorting relative to the total number of traders.

Answer: 1

The Short Interest Ratio compares the number of shorts held by the bears with the "free float" in any given stock. The free float is the number of shares available for shorting—the total number issued by the company minus restricted stock granted to executives, held by "strategic shareholders," and insiders' holdings. Brokers report the number of shares that have been shorted and not covered. If you divide that number by the total free float, you'll have the Short Interest Ratio, reflecting the intensity of shorting in any given stock.

Question 100—Trading the Short Interest Ratio

Tracking the Short Interest Ratio can help a trader in all of the following ways, except:

1. A rising Short Interest Ratio confirms a downtrend.
2. A Short Interest Ratio over 20% warns that the stock is liable to have a sharp rally.
3. A Short Interest Ratio under 10% means that shorting is relatively safe.
4. A falling Short Interest Ratio calls for a break in the stock.

Answer: 4

When the Short Interest Ratio rises, it shows that bears are becoming angrier and louder. Every short position must eventually be covered, and those short-covering rallies are notorious for their speed. As an estimate, a Short Ratio of less than 10% is likely to be tolerable, while a reading of over 20% marks a suspiciously large crowd of short-sellers. The Short Interest Ratio tends to increase as the stock slides and more bears join the party. The Short Interest Ratio tends to decline during the uptrend; such uptrends can last for a long time.

Question 101—Markets Need Shorting

Which of the following markets could exist without shorting?

1. Stocks
2. Futures
3. Options
4. Forex

Answer: 1

While only a small minority of stock traders sell short, the volume of shorting in futures, options, or forex is exactly equal to that of buying. For every contract bought there is a contract sold short—total long and short positions are absolutely equal in every trading vehicle except stocks.

Question 102—Who Shorts Futures

Most shorts in the futures markets are being held by:

1. Public speculators
2. Commercials or hedgers
3. CFTC
4. Hedge funds

Answer: 2

Most shorts in most futures markets are held by the commercials or hedgers who are the true insiders. For example, a major agribusiness may sell wheat futures to lock in a good price for a harvest that has not yet been gathered. But that is only part of the game. Any hedger worth its salt runs its futures division as a profit center and not merely as a price insurance office. They expect to make money on those positions.

Question 103—Shorting Futures

Find the incorrect statement about shorting futures:

1. A seller enters into a binding contract for future delivery.
2. The floor for a commodity price is defined by its cost of production.
3. Insider trading is illegal in futures.
4. The ceiling for a commodity price is defined by the cost of substitution.

Answer: 3

When you trade futures, you enter into binding contracts for a future purchase or sale of a commodity. All trades are backed by margin deposits on both sides. Futures, unlike stocks, have natural floors and ceilings. The cost of production creates a floor and the price of substitution a ceiling. Those levels, however, are somewhat flexible rather than totally rigid. In futures, there is no prohibition against insider trading because hedgers are the true insiders. You can track their behavior through "commitments of traders" reports, regularly published by CFTC.

Question 104—Long Rallies and Sharp Breaks

What is the main factor that makes many commodities prone to steady increases, punctuated by sharp declines?

1. Carrying charges
2. Manipulation
3. Seasonal factors
4. Cost of substitution

Answer: 1

Commodities incur carrying charges, as the cost of storing, financing, and insuring them gets worked into their prices. As all of these charges keep adding up month after month, prices could gradually climb to unrealistic heights. What happens instead is that relatively slow and steady price increases get punctuated by brief violent drops, returning prices to realistic levels—and then the process begins again.

Question 105—Writing Options

What is the main reason that options writing is much more profitable than buying?

1. The time value of options
2. Most buyers are undercapitalized.
3. Options move differently that stocks.
4. Most buyers are beginners.

Answer: 1

The key difference between options and stocks is that options are wasting assets. While all the factors listed in the question contribute to option buyers' mortality, the wasting time value of options is the most important among them. As the clock keeps ticking towards option expiration, it reduces the value of an option: the buyer keeps losing money, while the writer (seller) is more and more secure in his possession of the money received from the buyer.

Question 106—Writing Covered Options

What is the main disadvantage of writing covered options?

1. If the stock stays flat, you will have no capital gain in it.
2. If the stock falls, your long position will lose value.
3. If the stock rises above the exercise price, it will be called away.
4. Covered writing requires large capital.

Answer: 4

If the stock stays relatively flat and does not reach the option's exercise price, you will pocket the premium, boosting your total return. If the stock falls, you will also pocket the premium, cushioning the fall of your stock. If the stock rises above the option exercise price, it will be called away. You'll keep the premium in addition to the capital gain from the purchase price of the stock to the exercise level. Since there is a big universe of interesting stocks, you can take your freed-up capital and look for new opportunities. The fact that one needs substantial capital to purchase shares against which to write options in a large enough size to make financial sense, prevents most traders from getting into this business.

Question 107—Naked vs. Covered Writing

What is the main difference between naked and covered options writing?

1. Trade duration
2. How the trades are backed
3. Trade size
4. The analytic techniques

Answer: 2

While conservative investors write covered calls against their stocks, naked writers create options out of thin air, backed only by their cash. This backing for the trades—either by shares or cash—is the key difference between covered and naked writing. The differences in other areas are minimal or non-existent.

Question 108—The Demands of Naked Writing

The greatest demand that naked writing of options places on traders is:

1. Cash
2. Trading ideas
3. Discipline
4. Timing

Answer: 3

Naked writers walk a narrow line, protected only by their cash and skill; they need to be absolutely disciplined in taking profits or cutting losses. You cannot write options without sufficient cash, and you need to have good ideas and good timing. Even if you are excellent in those areas, you must have perfect discipline to succeed.

Question 109—Brokers Against Traders

In the following list of venues for trading forex, where does a broker's profit usually depend on a trader's loss?

1. The interbank market
2. Currency futures
3. Holding foreign cash
4. Forex trading houses

Answer: 4

Most forex houses operate as bucket shops—rather than transmit your orders for execution, they take the opposite side of any trade, whatever you want to trade, either long or short. When you trade in the interbank market, buy or sell currency futures, or simply exchange cash, a brokerage house does not care whether you make or lose money. They execute your orders and collect commissions. On the other hand, most forex shops bet against their own customers on every trade. When their clients lose, the shops make money.

Question 110—Forex Market

Which of the following does not apply to the forex market?

1. It is one of the most trending markets on a long-term basis.
2. It is largely driven by the fundamentals of government policies.
3. It is easy to plan and enter trades in forex.
4. It trades essentially 24/7.

Answer: 3

Any time a salesman tells you that something is easy in the market, run the other way! Yes, forex trades 24/7, but this means that a trade which you have carefully planned may come together on the other side of the globe while you are asleep. Once a currency gets into a major trend, whether up or down, it might stay in it for years, due to the fact that in the long run the value of a country's currency depends on government policies.

Question 111—Learning to Become a Better Trader

The most important factor in learning to become a better trader is:

1. Researching the market
2. Keeping good records
3. Finessing your entry and exit techniques
4. Luck

Answer: 2

The single most important factor in your long-term success or failure is the quality of your records. Keeping and reviewing them will allow you to improve your research and trading techniques. The harder you work, the luckier you'll become.

Question 112—Trading Signals of Force Index

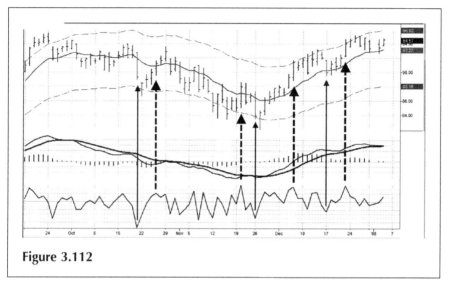

Figure 3.112

On the chart above, you can see that the downspikes of Force Index (marked by solid arrows) tend to be followed by price bottoms the following day. The chart also shows that the upspikes of Force Index (marked by dashed arrows) tend to be followed by the continuation of the uptrend rather than a top. These differences indicate that:

1. This indicator works only in downtrends.
2. This indicator works only in uptrends.
3. Uptrends and downtrends are not symmetrical and have to be traded differently.
4. One can base a trade on a single indicator in a bear market.

Answer: 3

Uptrends are driven by greed and tend to last longer. Downtrends are driven by fear; they tend to be more intense but last a shorter time. This essential asymmetry of tops and bottoms means that while the general principles of chart reading remain the same, selling short requires sharper timing. A single indicator is never enough; a trader must look for confirming signs—for example, a spike occurring while the price hits the channel line. A short-seller cannot afford to give his trade more time to "work out."

Question 113—False Breakouts and Divergences

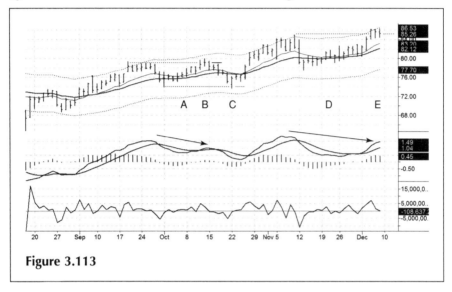

Figure 3.113

Please match the letters on the chart to the following descriptions:

1. False breakouts
2. Divergences

> **Answer:** 1. **B, C,** and **E**
> 2. **A** and **D**

Tops and bottoms tend to be asymmetrical. Technical signals, such as false breakouts and divergences can provide signals to sell short as well as to buy, but the timing is likely to be different. Notice, for example, how a false downside breakout was over in a day, while each of the false upside breakouts lasted for three days. It is harder to place stops on shorts; two days beyond the right edge of this chart the stock stabbed to a new high before collapsing; a tight stop would have led to a whipsaw.

Question 114—Shorting and Covering Signals

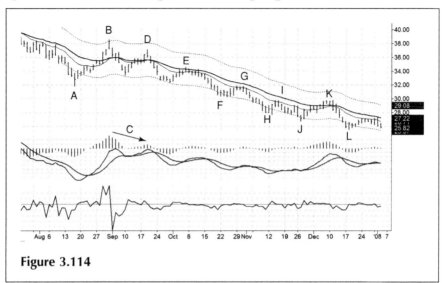

Figure 3.114

Please match the letters on the chart to the following descriptions:

1. Pullbacks to value
2. Undervalued zone
3. Kangaroo tails
4. Divergences

> **Answer:** 1. E, G, I, and K
>   2. A, F, H, J, and L
>   3. A, B, and D
>   4. C

When you find a stock traveling in a well-defined down-sloping channel, you can sell short at or above value, as defined by the moving averages. You can cover whenever prices fall to or below the undervalued area, defined by the lower channel line. Like many other patterns, kangaroo tails work near the bottoms as well as near the tops.

Question 115—Shorting Tactics

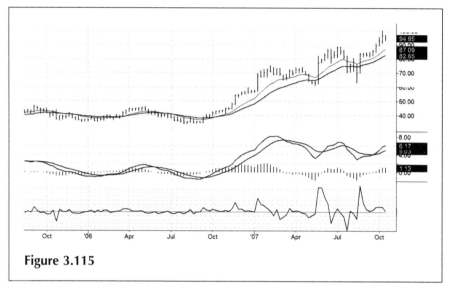

Figure 3.115

Please select the tactic to follow for the next few weeks at the right edge of the chart:

1. The trend is up—buy here, near $94.95.
2. The trend is up—buy on a breakout above the recent peak of $100.50.
3. The Impulse system turned Blue with the downtick of MACD—sell short, with the target of $87, near the fast EMA.
4. The Impulse system turned Blue—sell short with a target of $81, near the slow EMA.

Answer: 3

This stock is in a powerful bull market, but no trend goes in a straight line. The place to buy is near value, but now prices are overextended above value. With the MACD-Histogram ticking down and the Impulse turning blue, while the Force Index is showing a bearish divergence, shorting becomes an attractive option. The fast EMA is a realistic target; if and when prices approach that target, a trader may re-evaluate the situation and decide whether to cover or to hold.

GRADING YOUR ANSWERS

If a question requires only one answer, you earn a point by answering it correctly. If a question requires several answers (for example, "Which two of the following four statements are correct?"), rate your answer proportionately. If you answer both correctly, give yourself a point, but if only one, then half a point.

25–29: Excellent. You have a good grasp of selling short. The markets await you. Be sure to keep good records in order to learn from your experience.

21–24: Fairly good. Successful trading demands top performance. Look up the answers to the questions you've missed, review them, and retake the test in a few days before moving on to the next section.

Below 21: Alarm! Being below the top third in your answers is a sign of great danger in trading. Professional traders are waiting for you in the markets, ready to take your money. Before you do battle with them, you must bring yourself up to speed. Please study the third section of *Sell and Sell Short* and retake the test. If your grade remains low on the second pass, look up the books recommended in that section and study them. Avoid shorting until your performance on this test has improved.

What's Next?

Now that you have worked through this *Study Guide*, what should be your next step or steps?

I hope that the key concepts in *Sell and Sell Short* and in this *Study Guide* have become ingrained in your mind:

- Every trade deserves a plan: when you decide to buy, you need to plan when and where to sell. A trade without a selling plan is a gamble.

- The markets move down as well as up: learn to sell short and take advantage of the downmoves instead of feeling victimized by them.

- Practice money management: risk control is just as important as market analysis. Never overtrade, and when in doubt, trade a smaller size or stand aside.

- Keep a trading diary and keep reviewing it in order to learn from your successes and failures.

Now start implementing the ideas of *Sell and Sell Short* and of this *Study Guide* in your own trading. Please do not rush—so many beginners make the fatal mistake of trying to make a lot of money in a hurry. They put on trades that are too large for their accounts, become stiff with tension, their decision-making suffers, and they lose. If you learn to trade a 10-share lot, you will know when the time is right to move up to 50-share lots, and then to 100 shares, to 1,000, and even 10,000 shares at a clip. Learn to trade a small size and move up slowly. Quickly reduce trade size after a string of losses to protect yourself.

131

Anyone can buy a stock, but you must sell and sell well to book a profit or cut a loss. Once you learn how to sell, move on to short-selling to take advantage of the markets' downmoves.

Trading is an old man's game, and now increasingly a woman's. Experience matters, but to profit from it you have to stay in the game long enough. You need to set up a system of money management and record-keeping to survive the dangerous early stages of growth and development. At the risk of repeating myself, I'll say yet again: "Show me a trader with good records, and I will show you a good trader."

If you would like to stay in touch, please visit www.elder.com and sign up for our free newsletter. About once a month I put my thoughts into an e-mail and send it out to clients and friends. The topics of selling and shorting often emerge in those letters.

Trading the markets is the most exciting and engrossing pursuit. I wish you success.

Dr. Alexander Elder
New York City, 2008

About the Author

Alexander Elder, M.D., is a professional trader and a teacher of traders. He is the author of *Trading for a Living* and the *Study Guide for Trading for a Living*, considered modern classics among traders. First published in 1993, these international best-sellers have been translated into more than a dozen languages and are being used to educate traders around the world. His *Come into My Trading Room: A Complete Guide to Trading* was named a 2002 Barron's Book of the Year. His *Entries & Exits: Visits to 16 Trading Rooms* was named a 2007 SFO Magazine Book of the Year. He also wrote *Rubles to Dollars: Making Money on Russia's Exploding Financial Frontier* and *Straying from the Flock: Travels in New Zealand.*

Dr. Elder was born in Leningrad and grew up in Estonia, where he entered medical school at the age of 16. At 23, while working as a ship's doctor, he jumped a Soviet ship in Africa and received political asylum in the United States. He worked as a psychiatrist in New York City and taught at Columbia University. His experience as a psychiatrist provided him with unique insight into the psychology of trading. Dr. Elder's books, articles, and reviews have established him as one of today's leading experts on trading. Many of his own trades are featured in this book.

Dr. Elder is the originator of Traders' Camps—week-long classes for traders. He is also the founder of the Spike group, whose members are professional and semi-professional traders. They share their best stock picks each week in competition for prizes among themselves. Dr. Elder continues to trade, conducts webinars for traders, and is a sought-after speaker at conferences in the U.S. and abroad. Readers of this book are welcome to request a free subscription to his electronic newsletter by contacting his office:

elder.com
PO Box 20555, Columbus Circle Station
New York, NY 10023, USA
Tel. 718.507.1033
e-mail: info@elder.com
website: www.elder.com